"Inside this book, Del Duduit brings out obstacles faced by some of the most recognizable names in the National Football League. And how did they get through their trials? The same way I do. We let Christ fight our battles."

—William White, retired NFL player

"Football fans will love *First Down Devotions* from Del Duduit. In addition to faith-filled testimony from some of our favorite players, Del offers practical, spiritually sound guidance for living effective Christian lives. A must-read."

—Bruce A. Stewart, award-winning author of
Sing Me Something Happy.

"Like a solid run up the middle, *First Down Devotions* will help you establish your spiritual ground game that will lead you to victory. Each devotional gives an inspirational boost you can turn to for an effective game plan and a fresh set of downs. Pick a chapter. Any chapter. Each devotion goes good with a cup of coffee."

—Mark W. Prasek, president, By His Grace Ministries,
and founder, Patriot Journalist Network

"Del Duduit not only takes us into the lives of some of the best professional football players in the NFL, but more importantly, he takes us into their godly lives of faith, their convictions, and what it means to live their lives for the Lord."

—Cynthia S. Brown, author and freelance writer

"I coached youth football for several years, teaching character more than skill. Gridiron heroes are idolized for their on-the-field exploits. *First Down Devotions* shows us how these players' reliance on God is what propels them to success on and off the field. What great examples for our young people, for all people."

—J. D. Wininger, author and speaker

"*First Down Devotions* is not just for football lovers. As a business owner, speaker, and writer, I gleaned team building and leadership tools from this impactful devotional filled with inspiring stories from well-loved athletes. These godly players give our youth hope and an example of living for Christ. I highly recommend *First Down Devotions* for sports teams, pastors, leaders, and anyone who wants to grow closer to God."

—Cherrilynn Bisbano, speaker, writer, and
founder of The Write Proposal

"Del Duduit's *First Down Devotions* gives us insight into what truly makes a champion a champion. Through the testimonies and the illustrations Del uses, he makes the devotionals applicable to the reader, giving this book the power to be life changing. The truths of these devotions teach the reader what it means to take the field for faith each day. Exceptional book by an incredible author."

—Andy Clapp, pastor and author

"*First Down Devotions* is a showcase of Del's uncanny gift of connecting with athletes and sharing the raw stories of their faith journey. His master storytelling coupled with his own humble faith makes this a winner for anyone desiring to live a life of freedom and triumph."

—Rhonda Krill, founder and president,
One Christian Voice

FIRST DOWN DEVOTIONS

DEVOTIONS

INSPIRATION FROM NFL'S BEST

DEL DUDUIT

An imprint of Iron Stream Media
Birmingham, Alabama

Other books in the Stars of the Faith Series

Dugout Devotions: Inspirational Hits from MLB's Best

Iron Stream Books
5184 Caldwell Mill Rd.
St. 204-221
Hoover, AL 35244
IronStreamMedia.com
Iron Stream Books is an imprint of Iron Stream Media

Iron Stream Media serves its authors as they express their views, which may not express the views of the publisher. Portions of the articles included in this book may have been previously published. The profiles included are chosen solely by the author.

Library of Congress Cataloging-in-Publication Data

Names: Duduit, Del, 1966- editor.
Title: First down devotions : inspiration from NFL's best / [edited by] Del Duduit.
Description: First [edition]. | Birmingham : Iron Stream Books, 2019.
Identifiers: LCCN 2019006105 | ISBN 9781563092312 (permabind)
Subjects: LCSH: Christian life. | Spiritual life—Christianity. | Football players—Religious life.
Classification: LCC BV4501.3 .F56929 2019 | DDC 242/.68—dc23
LC record available at https://lccn.loc.gov/2019006105

Copyright information continues on page 143.

ISBN-13: 978-1-56309-231-2
Ebook ISBN: 978-1-56309-155-1

1 2 3 4 5—23 22 21 20 19

This book is dedicated to my youngest son, Eli.

Football is a game of passion and emotion, and you always displayed this as a young man. From your days of travel baseball to junior high football to serving as a senior captain in basketball and baseball, you have always displayed unbridled enthusiasm.

You wore it on your sleeve. Everyone knew when you were happy or when you were frustrated.

You carried this passion all through high school and college where you received many awards for your leadership.

I recall the times when I coached you in peewee football and how much you wanted to win every game. The same was true in high school baseball when you always led the team in prayer.

On the diamond, you earned the hustle award and most valuable player award twice because you gave 100 percent to your team. And the fact your coach selected you to serve as team captain three out of four years told me a lot about your desire to excel.

Today, your passion still shines, but in other ways.

Your mom and I are always blessed to see you praise and worship your Lord, and your fire also shows when you preach the gospel.

You are no longer a player on the field of athletics but in life. You are an example of a wonderful son and husband, and we know someday you will be an excellent father.

Keep the passion burning so all those around you will be guided by your leadership. Thanks for being a great son to me and a shining example of how to stand firm on your beliefs.

Dad

CONTENTS

The following people played a vital role in the completion of this book. I would like to personally thank them.

My wife Angie for being my first editor and supporting me through the proposal process.

My agent Cyle Young for his assistance in getting this book in front of the right people and for contributing devotionals for this book.

Mark Richard, editor of the *Portsmouth Daily Times* in Portsmouth, Ohio, for assisting with media credentials.

Hope Comer, publisher of the *Portsmouth Daily Times*, for her support.

William White for writing the foreword and for being a friend.

Michelle Medlock Adams for contributing devotionals.

Ryan Farr for contributing devotionals.

Beckie Lindsey for contributing devotionals.

Scott McCausey for contributing devotionals.

Bill Watkins for the inspiration to write this series.

Mark Householder, Ed Uszynski, Brian Smith, and Athletes in Action for providing support and opportunities.

Ramona Richards and John Herring with Iron Stream Media for this opportunity.

Reagan Jackson, one of my editors at Iron Stream Media, for putting up with me.

And God, for making this all possible.

FOREWORD

One of my biggest honors as a professional football player was to start for the Atlanta Falcons in Super Bowl XXXIII.

Years of practice and dedication went into that moment. Many of those countless hours were spent at Ohio State University, where I played for the Buckeyes. At Ohio State, I learned valuable lessons about teamwork, the game of football, and how life is not just about me. My six years with the Detroit Lions, three years with the Kansas City Chiefs, and two seasons in Atlanta also prepared me for that special moment—the Super Bowl, my final NFL game.

Football has been wonderful to me. It allowed me to physically perform at the highest level, one that only a few athletes achieve. Football also provided for my family and blessed me with great friendships. The sport taught me how to be humble, and it gave me the important understanding that failure is not failure until you quit. In football, you must stay positive with a next-man-up attitude. Life is the same.

I am fine with people referring to me as a Buckeye and a player in the NFL because that was a huge part of my life. I played football for twenty years. However, football is not my legacy. The foundation of my life is Jesus Christ. My ultimate goal is for people to see that Christ is real, that He lives within me, and that He can live within everyone if they allow it.

We all have challenges in life, and mine are different every day. I'm no longer testing myself against the best football players in the world, but God has now challenged me in a special way. He has chosen me to demonstrate his grace in my fight against ALS, an incurable neurological disease that I was diagnosed with in 2016.

I don't question why God chose me for this challenge. Instead, I think often about the Scripture verse Romans 8:28: "And we know that all things work together for good to those who love God, to those who are called according to His purpose" (NKJV).

My diagnosis is only part of all things that are happening in God's plan. This is part of His plan for me. Now, instead of playing football, I'm on Team Jesus. I know I must play my new role so we all win.

Inside this book, Del Duduit brings out other obstacles faced by some of the most recognizable names in the National Football League. And how did they get through their trials? The same way I do. We let Christ fight our battles.

He also includes wonderful stories of hope and dedication gleaned from interviews with Andy Dalton and Adam Vinatieri. You will be encouraged when you read about Anthony Muñoz and his decision to follow Christ and how Benjamin Watson identifies as a believer and not just a player.

You will also get a chance to read my testimony.

Each chapter will inspire you to dig deeper in your walk as a follower of the Lord as told through these athletes.

My life's role as a football player has ended, but my true role is explained in Philippians 1:21: "For to me, to live is Christ and to die is gain."

My journey here on earth is to fulfill the plans God has for me. When I die, I win because I get to spend eternity with my Heavenly Father.

My life is in the hands of God, and I pray you find the encouragement you need in this book to play on the divine winning Super Bowl team for Him.

God bless,
William White
Safety for the Atlanta Falcons

DAY 1
IDENTIFY WITH GOD

Benjamin Watson
Super Bowl Champion and Tight End
New Orleans Saints

By Del Duduit

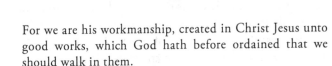

For we are his workmanship, created in Christ Jesus unto good works, which God hath before ordained that we should walk in them.

—Ephesians 2:10 KJV

Benjamin Watson knows how to play the game of football.

The six-foot-three, 250-pound tight end won a Super Bowl ring with the New England Patriots in 2004 and caught five hundred passes by the start of the 2018 season.

He was a first-round draft pick by New England but spent a lot of time on the injured reserved list. He worked hard to come back and wanted to be an impactful player.

Football was his life. The sport dominated his thoughts, and he strived for perfection on the field.

"There were times, especially in my career, when my identity was wrapped up in football," he said. "It's all I was. I worked out, watched film, studied all the time. Football was my whole life."

The sport demands a lot of time in order to be successful. Along with professional football comes a lavish lifestyle for some. Many of the players are treated like royalty by the team and adored by fans. All needs are met beyond measure, and the players want for nothing.

"We are supposed to be excellent at what we do, and I wanted to be excellent," Benjamin said. "We give our all to our job, and we are paid a lot of money to be good."

But at what expense?

Who did he serve? What was his identity?

"God gives us all different talents, and we should always give our all to those things," he said. "But I was taking what was going on in my physical journey with football and transferring it over to my spiritual walk, and that is not where we need to be."

Benjamin realized the Lord called him to do even bigger and better things than professional football, which he does well.

He became vocal on social issues and used his platform to glorify God and stand up for what he perceives is right, including releasing a book he coauthored called *Under Our Skin: Getting Real About Race. Getting Free from the Fears and Frustrations that Divide Us.*

On January 27, 2017, he was a featured speaker at the National March for Life in Washington, DC, where he spoke to thousands about the sanctity of life and made his voice clear he is against abortion.

In 2018, he won the Bart Starr Award presented by Athletes in Action for his outstanding community service and his willingness to lift up and glorify the name of Jesus Christ.

His journey has taken him from football player in the NFL to also serve as an ambassador for the Lord.

> I am crucified with Christ; nevertheless I live; yet not I, but Christ liveth in me: and the life which I now live in the flesh I live by the faith of the Son of God, who loved me, and gave himself for me.
>
> —Galatians 2:20 KJV

Huddle Up

There is nothing wrong with success in the workplace. Like Benjamin said, we should strive to be the best at what we do. That is how God made us. If we slack off on the job, we steal from our company, and that is not right. There is, however, a fine line. In today's society, people strive to get ahead and climb the ladder, and it's easy to make your job or hobby number one. But is that who you are? When your time is over, how will people remember you? Will those who know you say you were a fantastic banker? Will they recall you as someone who worked all the time? Or will they first say you were a man of God? Who are you? Who do you want to be?

Cross the Goal Line

You don't live to work. You work to live. Put in an honest day's labor and be compensated in a fair way. Some occupations demand more time, but they don't have to dominate your identity. Benjamin is a football player by trade. But he is considered a godly man who speaks out and witnesses for his

Savior. He talks in front of audiences about his faith and has found a way to use his platform to publically brag on the Lord. Consider your legacy and who you serve. Here are some ways to be successful in your job and still have a championship witness:

- Family comes first: This is your number-one priority. If your daughter has a recital in the evening and you have a report due to your boss the next day, find time later to prepare. If your son is scheduled to be honored at an event, be there. And if your wife wants to go out on a date, put the work on hold. Make time for those who are important in your life. There are times when work must come first, but it should not be your priority all the time.
- Tithe faithfully: You are commanded to give a portion of what you earn back to God. After all, He gave you the job and income you have. "Honor the LORD with thy substance, and with the firstfruits of all thine increase" (Proverbs 3:9 KJV).
- Give of your time: Volunteer at a charity of your choice on a regular basis. Become involved with a nonprofit organization or even take a mission trip.
- Support others in times of need: A simple card dropped in the mail or a text to a friend who may have lost a loved one is a sign of support. People will remember you took time to think of them and will not view you as a person who works nonstop. "Wherefore comfort yourselves together, and edify one another, even as also ye do" (1 Thessalonians 5:11 KJV).

- Minister in your own way: You don't have to be a pastor to have a ministry. Maybe write a blog or contribute monthly columns to your newspaper. You don't need recognition for what you do for God all the time. A faithful ministry does not go unnoticed. Consider regular visits to those who are sick or to terminal patients in hospice. Take food to nurses on the night shift and pray with them. There are many ways you can have an impact for the Lord.

You are a child of God. Find ways to be identified with the King of kings. Benjamin is a professional athlete. But that is not the only way people think of him. He has established his name as a player of the Lord's team. Who are you?

DAY 2
BE DEDICATED TO YOUR TEAM

Andy Dalton
Pro-Bowl Quarterback
Cincinnati Bengals

By Del Duduit

Let love and faithfulness never leave you; bind them around
your neck, write them on the tablet of your heart.
—Proverbs 3:3

Cincinnati Bengals quarterback Andy Dalton has his priorities in order. He practices long hours at his craft, dedicates time to give back to the community, helps those around him improve, and lets the whole world know he's married—even when he's on the football field.

For a few justifiable reasons, many football players do not wear a wedding band when they go to work. There is a risk of injury should the symbol of love be caught or snagged on a jersey. A player might have his finger broken or may lose the valuable token on the field of play.

One of Andy's fellow alumni from Texas Christian University cofounded Qalo, a company that makes silicone rings for active athletes to wear. For Dalton, these were a perfect fit. The Pro-Bowl signal caller likes the concept so much he wears the bands everywhere he goes—even into the huddle.

"I am married, and to wear a ring and not have to worry about it getting damaged is nice," he said. "I want everyone to know I'm married, and I have no reason to take this ring off."

He even color coordinates with his uniforms. When the team is on the road in white jerseys, he puts on the white Qalo. At home, the black one makes an appearance. He wants to show Cincinnati, his colleagues, and the world he is off the market, even when he's on the field.

> He who finds a wife finds what is good and receives favor from the LORD.
>
> —Proverbs 18:22

If you are married, do those around you know you are committed? Do you wear your ring if you can? Are you dedicated?

In the Huddle

For most married men, this is a no-brainer. Of course you wear your ring all the time. There might be instances when you take it off, for example when you do yard work or repair the car. You don't want to lose the symbol of your love or damage it when you do work around the house. But for the most part, it's a normal and expected part of your wardrobe. But what if you take a road trip away from home? Maybe you and your spouse had a fight or you feel you no longer have "excitement" in your marriage. Or perhaps you have allowed a door to open that should have stayed closed. Maybe a former girlfriend has reached out to you on social media and wants to reconnect because her marriage failed. Will you be faithful to your wife?

Cross the Goal Line

You know the right call to make. In your heart, there is no question. There are no excuses. Be faithful to your spouse no matter the circumstance. If there is a trust issue, step up in the pocket and deliver a pass to the right receiver. Be a man with integrity. Stay focused on the task at hand and stick to your game plan. Victory is just in sight. The devil's main target is the family. If he can intercept a pass or tackle you in the backfield, he will be thrilled. Here are some suggestions on how to show you are dedicated to your spouse and continue to make your obligation to your household a top priority:

- Show her love: Do your best to nurture and cherish your wife. There might be circumstances outside your control, but always show love. Protect her from harm, show her tenderness, and be responsive to her needs. "Husbands, love your wives, just as Christ loved the church and gave himself up for her" (Ephesians 5:25).
- Show her respect: Honoring your wife is always important, but even more so if you have children. Little ears and eyes hear and see what goes on in the home, and you must model the example for them to follow someday when they have families of their own. A man of faith should always esteem his wife.
- Show her affection: Hold her hand in public or cuddle with her on the couch. The tough guy or bad-boy image is not so attractive as the movies might make it appear. Your spouse may not need 100 percent of your attention, but she does need affection. Touch is important to her.

- Show her leadership: God expects the man of the home to lead by example. This does not give you the authority to be a dictator. Pray and ask for God's guidance. Share decisions with your spouse and be flexible, yet stick to your convictions. Take everyone's circumstances into consideration before a decision is reached. "Kings detest wrongdoing, for a throne is established through righteousness" (Proverbs 16:12).
- Show her you care: Examine and look at her needs and put them in front of your own. "In this same way, husbands ought to love their wives as their own bodies. He who loves his wife loves himself" (Ephesians 5:28).
- Show her attention: You may think small acts of kindness are insignificant, but they might be major to her. A simple call or text throughout the day or a surprise gift at the office will let her know you care. Help around the house with dishes or take a turn in the laundry room. Let her know you are still attracted to her and always will be.
- Show her devotion: This is true in all situations—good times and bad. There might be emotional, physical, or financial issues to deal with in life. Christ loves the church and you so much He sacrificed His life for mankind. Honor your spouse, and let her know you are willing to do whatever it takes to defend her. Stay faithful and true. Wear your ring and take pride in your marriage. "A wife of noble character who can find? She is worth far more than rubies" (Proverbs 31:10).

When you take a stand and let everyone know you are married and proud to be with your partner for life, doubt and insecurity will flee. Andy steps up and delivers in the clutch while thousands of people watch the football sail through the air and into the grasp of a receiver for a score. At the same time, they see the ring on his hand and know he's a committed and dedicated husband.

DAY 3
WHEN GOD SENDS A SONG

Ben Roethlisberger
Super Bowl Champion Quarterback
Pittsburgh Steelers

By Del Duduit

Speaking to yourselves in psalms and hymns and spiritual
songs, singing and making melody in your heart to the Lord.
—Ephesians 5:19 KJV

By many standards, Pittsburgh Steelers quarterback Ben
Roethlisberger appeared to have it all. NFL fans adored
him in the Steel City.

His followers were unaware he faced some difficult personal challenges, and they did not know Satan had targeted
him for destruction. If Big Ben could fall, then the devil
would be excited. He loves when men of faith stumble in
their walk with Christ. But even more, he gets a kick when
he is able to shatter a man's witness in front of the entire
world. The enemy rejoices when he can bring down popular
people and toss their witness for the Lord out the window.

He almost succeeded.

Ben's résumé speaks for itself. Two Super Bowl rings, six
Pro-Bowl appearances, and one Rookie of the Year award.
When Pittsburgh made the playoffs, the team had excellent

odds to reach the Super Bowl because of his leadership on the field.

Between 2006 and 2010, Ben's personal life started to unravel. At the end of this period, the NFL suspended him for four games and ordered him to undergo professional behavioral evaluations. His world was on a downward spiral, and his life and reputation were at risk.

But he found the boost he needed when he listened to a song by TobyMac.

He was driving one day when the song "Lose My Soul" began to play on the radio. He had grown up in a small church in Lima, Ohio, and he knew the difference between right and wrong. The message contained in the popular tune opened his eyes to allow him to see the circumstances at stake.

"I just pulled over and started crying," Ben said. "That song came at a time when I needed to hear it. I thought to myself, I have it all, but I don't want to lose my soul."

Right there in his car, he prayed and reconnected with Christ, and he has been a wonderful role model for the kingdom ever since. He handled his problems by leaning on God for strength and forgiveness and turned the problems he created over to the Lord.

"My faith means everything to me," he added. "I play for Him first."

Sing unto him, sing psalms unto him: talk ye of all his wondrous works.

—Psalm 105:2 KJV

In the Huddle

Perhaps you are like Ben and have gone through some personal trials. Although God forgives you for what you have done, He expects you to make things right. The Savior of the World wants you to turn all your cares over to Him. This does not mean your problems will disappear, but you can count on Him to provide comfort and help you fight your battles. Are your troubles too difficult to handle alone? Have you put yourself in a terrible situation? There is hope in Christ.

Cross the Goal Line

In order for you to make a play and win in life's game, you must first know the devil's defensive strategy. Here are some ways to know your weaknesses and how to protect yourself.

- Admit you have a tendency to sin: We all do. You are no different. You are human and have desires of the flesh. Expect to be tempted by the forces of evil, and be prepared for the attacks. When you know your weaknesses, you can put a game plan in place to make you stronger. "But every man is tempted, when he is drawn away of his own lust, and enticed" (James 1:14 KJV).
- Get away from the wrong attractions: When you allow temptations to draw close, you are in trouble. You will be in a better place if you flee from them—don't try to handle these situations yourself. When Ben sees a blitz coming toward him, he does not stand in and fight the rushing linemen. He flees and jukes his way around them to escape and make the play.

- Know the Word of God: This is your playbook. All successful NFL players have to rely on the playbook in order to win. You are no different. Dive into the Bible and memorize Scripture to strengthen you when you are pressured by the devil. Jesus had to overcome temptation, and you are no different. You are subject to attacks because Satan knows you are weak and of the flesh. But if you have some go-to verses and stay in the Word of God, you will become stronger. "For the weapons of our warfare are not carnal, but mighty through God to the pulling down of strong holds" (2 Corinthians 10:4 KJV).

- Ask for strength and guidance: Seek God's assistance—this is not a sign of weakness but rather an admission you need help. A man gains strength when he is on his knees in prayer. When you continue in sin, you are at risk of death and destruction. Plead for forgiveness and help while you still can. Stay on the right path. You might encounter an unwanted detour but find your way back to the straight and narrow.

- Be accountable: Find some friends who will hold you up to a higher standard and pray for you. Choose three or four men you can meet with on a monthly basis to discuss any concerns you have in your life. Be accountable to them as your personal board of directors. In turn, you can do the same for them. "Iron sharpeneth iron; so a man sharpeneth the countenance of his friend" (Proverbs 27:17 KJV).

- Keep a song in your heart: A song reminded Ben that while he had the earthly pleasures of life, his soul was in jeopardy. Nothing is worth eternity in hell. When trials come your way—and they will—make sure you have a song to sing to remind you about the good things God has in store for you.

Ben said God works in mysterious ways. You might become distracted with temptations of this world, but if you are not careful, you will find yourself in a mess. Don't let this happen. Recognize how the defense is lined up, and make your call at the line of scrimmage accordingly. The devil wants your soul for a trophy. Stay with your game plan to win the biggest competition of them all.

DAY 4

COMPETITION MAKES COMRADES

Kirk Cousins
Quarterback
Minnesota Vikings

By Scott McCausey

Behold, how good and pleasant it is when brothers dwell in unity!

—Psalm 133:1 ESV

The score was tied at 31 between two powerhouse football teams: the Michigan State Spartans and the Wisconsin Badgers. The Spartans were 5-1 and ranked fifteenth in the nation, and the Badgers were 6-0, ranked fourth. The game was destined for overtime, with the Spartans possessing the ball at the Wisconsin forty-four-yard line with four seconds on the clock. The Spartans were positioned to throw a Hail Mary.

Kirk Cousins took the snap and scrambled to his right. The three-man Badger rush broke through the line as Kirk set his feet and heaved the ball toward the end zone. The pigskin sailed over the goal line, slipped through the hands of the defensive back, and bounced off the chest of a Spartan and into the hands of converted quarterback Keith Nichol. Keith contorted to his left and was mobbed by Badgers.

He was right at the goal line as the defenders pushed him back and tackled him around the one-yard line. The two officials stared at one another over the pile of players and signaled no touchdown, but the play was about to be reviewed.

Rewinding the timeline reveals a rivalry between Kirk and the teammate who caught his desperation pass, Keith Nichols. In 2009, these two superstar quarterbacks split time, as Coach Mark Dantonio simply couldn't settle on a starter.

"Our quarterback coach once shared he'd never been part of a team competition where both players were as talented as Keith and me," Kirk said. "When I first arrived, I competed with future Super Bowl MVP Nick Foles, and if Keith had won the job, he'd probably be in the NFL as well. All these inner team competitions caused me to question what was going on and if God really wanted me to play at Michigan State, but He had a plan, and it certainly wasn't the easiest thing for me. There are many times where I wondered if God could have given a smoother path, but as a result of the challenges, it readied me for the next level."

In the Huddle

President Franklin D. Roosevelt once said, "Competition has been shown to be useful up to a certain point and no further, but cooperation, which is the thing we must strive for today, begins where competition leaves off."

Competition takes place in many venues. You may find yourself competing for a position at a company, in school for the best grades, or to be a starter on a sports team. Healthy competition drives us to be better, which makes the team we are part of stronger. "Two are better than one, because they have a good reward for their toil. For if they fall, one will lift up his fellow" (Ecclesiastes 4:9–10 ESV).

Does competition stress you out or does it make you stronger? Do you draw closer to those you are competing with, understanding you are in this together?

Cross the Goal Line

Competition can bring out the best and the worst in people. We must remind ourselves of the goal to display God's kingdom here on earth. The following are some ways we can better achieve this together.

- Understand your strengths and weaknesses: When you find yourself locked in competition with a teammate, avoid anger, and instead develop positive character traits. Often you'll see the strengths of your teammate, which may point to a skill you can improve. Strengths you didn't know you possessed may also shine, revealing traits you can capitalize on.
- Keep perspective: We must ultimately remember the goal. "But seek first the kingdom of God and his righteousness, and all these things will be added to you" (Matthew 6:33 ESV). The *things* Matthew refers to are harmony in life's necessities. When we understand the competition, it adds value to ushering a kingdom perspective to our community, then we serve our Father. The proper vision will give a right attitude.
- Build up your team: Coach of the Green Bay Packers Vince Lombardi is often credited as saying, "Practice does not make perfect. Only perfect practice makes perfect." Practice is one of the most common places where the competition becomes heated. As the competitive juices begin to flow, keep your team in mind. If there's an inner squad scrimmage taking place, hurting your teammate due to

your drive and anger will not make the team better. Participate in drills and practice with team goals in mind. "Do your best to present yourself to God as one approved, a worker who has no need to be ashamed, rightly handling the word of truth" (2 Timothy 2:15 ESV).

- Engage: Have you found yourself in a rut? Sometimes we feel tired, lazy, or as though we are only going through the motions. Engaging in healthy competition can bring new energy and excitement into our lives and teach us new skills at the same time. "Whatever you do, work heartily, as for the Lord and not for men" (Colossians 3:23 ESV).
- We often avoid the competition to avoid injury. However, we can engage with a positive attitude so fun can be had. Competition doesn't have to be a bad thing, it can inspire to greatness.
- Create friendship not jealousy: Jealousy can lead to insecurity in the gifts God gives. We should never be insecure in these gifts, for the ultimate gift is Jesus Christ, our foundation for living. If you find yourself trapped in a jealous rage, seek Christ before engaging in competition. "For where jealousy and selfish ambition exist, there will be disorder and every vile practice" (James 3:16 ESV). A jealous heart breeds evil, which won't lead to friendship. As Kirk 'shared, the competition with Keith Nichols made them both better, not jealous or angry.
- "People say I competed against Keith. *Against* is the wrong word. I competed *with* Keith," Kirk said.

A crowded Spartan Stadium was quiet as the officials studied the tape of the last play. Did Keith cross the goal line?

"After further review, the runner did cross the goal line. Touchdown."

The stadium erupted in celebration as comrades hugged in thankfulness of the victory.

DAY 5
TAKE A KNEE

Adam Vinatieri
Kicker
Indianapolis Colts

By Michelle Medlock Adams

In all thy ways acknowledge him, and he shall direct thy paths.

—Proverbs 3:6 KJV

Indianapolis Colts kicker Adam Vinatieri hits both knees every morning in prayer to his Heavenly Father.

"That's a great place to start your life and your day," he said. "It's been a wonderful life . . . and it all started with me on my knees."

Adam gave his life to God back in college. He remembers that day well because he was at a crossroads, unsure of his next steps.

"Coming from a small Division II school, I didn't get drafted," he said. "I just remember dropping to my knees and asking God for direction. I prayed, 'If this is what You want me to do, let's go. If not, lead me in another direction.'"

Adam was willing to walk away from football if that was God's plan. In fact, at one point, he thought about going to medical school. But God didn't close the door to football;

He just took Adam on a path to the NFL by way of the World League of American Football.

After the New England Patriots' 1995 season, Coach Bill Parcells told his special-teams coach Mike Sweatman to find him a kicker. The Patriots' kicker Matt Bahr was coming off a less-than-great year, and Parcells wanted another option. Sweatman found three kickers, and one of them was Adam. At the time, Adam was unknown by most, playing for Amsterdam in the World League of American Football, but his coach Al Tanara knew him and was impressed by him. And, more importantly, Tanara knew Parcells. They were old coaching friends. So when Tanara highly recommended Adam, New England signed him.

Of course, he had to earn the right to stay in the NFL, and Parcells didn't go easy on him. It was touch and go his rookie season, but Adam impressed everyone—even the naysayers—after his performance against Dallas late in the season. Herschel Walker was running back at kickoff that day, and he broke through the Patriots' first line of defense. It looked like he would go all the way, but Adam tackled him hard. Parcells was quoted in a *Sports Illustrated* article as to how that game impacted the way he saw Adam: "We all looked at him a little different. It was like, 'This guy can play on our team any time.' He was in concrete after that."

Adam played for the Patriots for ten years and with the Indianapolis Colts for more than ten years. He's appeared in five Super Bowls, won four titles, and hit the game-winning kick as time expired in 2002 and 2004. As the current oldest active NFL player, he seems to get better with age.

Entering the 2018 season, Adam continues to impress and perform well, and Colts fans love him. While he enjoys the adoration of his community and his fans, he knows what really matters is the love of his Heavenly Father and his family.

"I'm not sure God cares too much about who wins football games, but He does care about me," he said, adding that his family provides the stability and joy that keeps him going. "For me, my rock is my family. No matter whether I have a tough day or not, my kids come running to me and give me a big hug. There's nothing better than that. It makes the day worthwhile and makes me forget about any problems."

Adam knows he is living a great life—waking up every day to play the sport he loves and coming home to an amazing family—but he also knows none of it would be possible without God. That's why he starts each day in prayer.

"I get out of the way and let Him do the planning," he said. "It's a wonderful life."

> This is the day that the LORD has made; we will rejoice and be glad in it.
>
> —Psalm 118:24 NKJV

In the Huddle

We often hear the phrase, "Let go and let God," but how many of us really practice this directive? By turning your life over to God and consistently starting your day with prayer, you put yourself in a position to succeed. John 10:27 says, "My sheep listen to my voice; I know them, and they follow me," but it's hard to distinguish God's voice from all the other competing voices if we don't spend time in prayer and in His Word every single day. Have you asked Jesus to be the Lord of your life? Do you talk to Him every day and allow Him to lead you?

Cross the Goal Line

Some people have trouble knowing how to pray; yet like Adam, we all need to pray daily in order hear from God and follow Him. Here are some tips to help you pray more effectively.

- Be specific with your requests: For example, don't just pray for peace in the family. Instead, pray: "God, I ask that You cause my children to love one another the way You love them. Let them always see the best in each other and enjoy spending time together."
- Use Scripture in your prayers: So, instead of praying, "Lord, I ask that You cause people to stop talking about me." Pray, "Lord, I thank You that no weapon formed against me shall prosper and every tongue that rises against me shall be stilled" (Isaiah 54:17). (Remember, Jeremiah 1:12 tells us God watches over His Word to fulfill it.)
- Believe when you pray: Don't simply say the words without believing God can really answer your requests. Pray expecting that when prayer is done within His will, God will fulfill His promises! After you've made your request known to God, thank Him for the desired result. Hebrews 11:6 (*The Message*) says, "It's impossible to please God apart from faith. And why? Because anyone who wants to approach God must believe both that he exists and that

he cares enough to respond to those who seek him." Also, check out Matthew 21:22 and Mark 11:24.

- Pray in Jesus' name: Some have prayed, "For Jesus' sake," and, "All God's people said amen," to close their prayers, but the Bible clearly tells us to pray in Jesus' name. In John 16:23 (NKJV), Jesus says: "And in that day you will ask Me nothing. Most assuredly, I say to you, whatever you ask the Father in My name He will give you."

Follow Adam's example—start each morning in prayer. Allow God to guide your steps and trust Him with your future. That's the only way to have a wonderful life.

DAY 6
TELL YOUR FRIENDS ABOUT
THE GOSPEL

Anthony Muñoz
Hall of Fame Tackle
Cincinnati Bengals

By Del Duduit

Walk in wisdom toward outsiders, making the best use
of the time. Let your speech always be gracious, seasoned
with salt, so that you may know how you ought to answer
each person.

—Colossians 4:5–6 ESV

Anthony Muñoz was a freshman in college when he heard
about the gospel of Jesus Christ.

How can this be? A popular athlete in high school, he
lived in Southern California among millions of people. But
it's true.

"I never heard about Christ until I went to college," he
said. "And once I heard about it, I knew I wanted to live
for the Lord."

Anthony, inducted into the Pro Football Hall of Fame in
1998, was a standout high school athlete and drew attention
from dozens of recruiters. He decided to accept a football
scholarship at the University of Southern California, where
he also played baseball.

One by one, God started to place people in his life that would expose the six foot six, 278-pounder to the gospel.

"I sat down with a staff member of Campus Crusade for Christ one day, and he started to ask me questions," he said. "He asked me about how my freshman year was going and about my grades and football."

Then the staffer inquired about his spiritual life.

"I said it was okay, but it was nonexistent," Anthony said. "I didn't know what he was talking about."

Then a teammate transferred into USC and began to witness to the future eleven-time Pro-Bowl selection.

"He started to share his faith with me, and so did his friends," he said. "They were everywhere."

The seeds were planted. After his freshman year, he went home on break and started to call on a young lady. On their first date, he accompanied her to her sister's wedding where her family shared their faith with Anthony.

"I started to think everyone was ganging up on me, because they were coming at me from all directions," he said with a laugh.

The couple married his sophomore year in April 1978. But that's not all that happened.

Six month later, they both gave their hearts to Christ at the same time. Today, they both live for the Lord and make an impact wherever they go.

"God used so many people to get to me," he said. "That's why I always tell about His mercy on me and His greatness. I want everyone to have the same Lord."

He went on to experience greatness on the gridiron. In 1991, he was named the NFL Man of the Year and was chosen to the 1980s All-Decade Team, among other highly acclaimed accomplishments.

"I love those awards, but being a Christian means more to me than anything," he said. "I love that Dee Dee and I were saved at the same time. We've made a great team all these years."

> That is, that we may be mutually encouraged by each other's faith, both yours and mine.
>
> —Romans 1:12 ESV

Huddle Up

Do your coworkers, friends, classmates, or neighbors know about your allegiance to the Lord? If they were asked to describe you, would the word *Christian* come to mind? Are there times when you have neglected to tell others about your relationship with the Master?

Cross the Goal Line

Don't worry. You are not alone. You have to juggle your professional obligations along with your responsibilities to share the gospel. In today's society, you have to be careful what you say because you could get fired or sued. But at the same time, you want to be a positive witness for the kingdom and invite others to experience true happiness and salvation. You don't have to be overbearing to get your point across. But those you interact with daily need to know where you stand, and it is simple and easy to share your faith with them. You don't have to part the Red Sea, but you can make your beliefs known in a way that will lead others to ask you about them and open doors for a conversation.

Live your life in a way that is consistent with the Bible. Your lifestyle should not leave people any doubts about your devotion to your church and the Lord. Live pure and set a good example to draw others to Him. If you are guilty of not representing Christ like you should, then start today to make a change. Ask the Lord for forgiveness, and dedicate your life to Him. "In the same way, let your light shine before others, so that they may see your good works and give glory to your Father who is in heaven" (Matthew 5:16 ESV).

- Identify yourself as a believer on social media: Every post does not have to include a Christian connotation, but once in a while is good. Post a Scripture verse you like or invite your friends to a service at your church. Change your profile to include the word *Christian*, and put a link to your church's website. This way, all your friends will know where you stand.
- Give back and volunteer: This is a great way to evangelize and encourage those who need help. You can do this once a month at a local food shelter or your church. Volunteer to help out on the bus ministry or in an area that interests you. When you become involved, you are accountable to your church leadership. "As each has received a gift, use it to serve one another, as good stewards of God's varied grace" (1 Peter 4:10 ESV).
- Display your faith: Place a Bible or some form of Christian symbol on your desk at work, on your binder at school, or on your car. Maybe you could use a coffee mug or wall calendar that includes Scripture. When your friends and

coworkers see this, it might be a conversation starter and give you the chance to tell them about your Savior.

- Invite a person to church each week: This can be done in person, through a private message on social media, or by text. Just a few simple words will suffice. "For truly, I say to you, whoever gives you a cup of water to drink because you belong to Christ will by no means lose his reward" (Mark 9:41 ESV).

Anthony was not exposed to the gospel until later in his teen years. God sent several people to make sure he knew about His saving grace. Make a point to say a kind word or do a good deed that will encourage someone. Plant a seed and watch it grow.

DAY 7
GET PAST THE SETBACKS AND
MACLIVE

Clinton McDonald
Defensive End
Oakland Raiders

By Cyle Young

> For everyone born of God overcomes the world. This is the
> victory that has overcome the world, even our faith.
> —1 John 5:4

Super Bowl champion Clinton McDonald knows what it's
like to work hard. In his nine years in the NFL he has
recorded 245 tackles and nineteen quarterback sacks while
playing for the Cincinnati Bengals, Seattle Seahawks,
Tampa Bay Buccaneers, and the Oakland Raiders.

Clinton's parents Larry and Bonnie McDonald both
served in the military before settling down in Jacksonville,
Arkansas, where Clinton would go on to be an All-State
football player. When sharing about his formative years in
Arkansas, Clinton is quick to share that his father inspired
him, "My father worked, and I never saw him get tired. Even
when he would get cut with a saw—never a tear or anything."

Clinton and his brother worked construction with their
father. The former Lockheed Martin flight instructor

allowed them to help him with "little grown-man jobs" like roofing, digging ditches, and demolition. Larry was Clinton's superhero, and he "wanted to be that tough" too. It's that same toughness that has allowed Clinton to endure the injuries, difficulties, and trials of life as a NFL football player.

In 2009, Clinton was selected in the last round of the NFL draft. Tony Pauline of TFY Draft called Clinton "one of the most underrated players of the draft." And Clinton continues to prove that statement to be true. He has out-lived the average lifespan of an NFL football career, and Clinton continues to overcome injury and setback and steadies himself as a valuable addition to any team.

He's been overcoming since a terrible 2006 car accident in which he survived despite not wearing a seatbelt. The car hydroplaned and flipped multiple times, totaling it. Clinton miraculously remained uninjured. At that moment, he knew there was a reason he survived: "God had something planned for me," and that was to be a servant to God and to others. And that's exactly how Clinton is using his NFL platform. The 2017 Walter Payton Man of the Year nominee has vowed to bring the light of the Lord into various Central Arkansas and Tampa, Florida, communities through his foundation, McDonald and Associates Collective Collaboration Light Into Darkness. Through his foundation, Clinton encourages people to MacLive, to go out everyday and uplift and encourage each other to be active and grow physically and spiritually. What a powerful message for everyone.

Who is it that overcomes the world? Only the one who believes that Jesus is the Son of God.

—1 John 5:5

In the Huddle

Do you MacLive? Do you invest your time to be active and grow physically and spiritually? Clinton uses the platform God gave him to reach into communities with the light of Christ, but you can do the same in your own community. You don't have to be a Super Bowl-winning football player to encourage and lift up others, but you may have to be spiritually tough. It isn't always easy to love people. Many times you'll have to sacrifice your own time and resources to leave a lasting impact on the world around you, but the end result—seeing lives changed by Christ—is so worth it.

Cross the Goal Line

You have to be tough to stand up against the enemies of Christ. They can attack you in many different ways that will keep you from living your life to the fullest but also cause you to miss out on the fulfillment of serving God and others—like Clinton McDonald does. Don't let self-doubt, setbacks, or an improper perspective keep you from being used by God. Those are only tools the enemy uses to keep you from experiencing the fullness of Christ.

- Trust God: Don't allow doubt to keep you from achieving the role God has called you to. God has a plan even when we can't see it. Clinton's terrible car accident allowed him to see God's bigger picture, but you can rest assured that God is always working His plan for you even when you don't recognize right away what God is doing. "See, I am doing a new thing! Now it springs up; do you not perceive it? I am making a way in the wilderness and streams in the wasteland" (Isaiah 43:19).

- Get a proper perspective: Clinton allowed God to use a car accident to get his attention. Look at your life long and hard, and evaluate whether or not God has been trying to speak to you through your circumstances. You will benefit from trying to see your life from God's perspective. Trust me, you don't want to have to miraculously survive a car accident before you realize God has a plan for your life. That's not the preferred way. "What, then, shall we say in response to these things? If God is for us, who can be against us?" (Romans 8:31).

- Overcome setbacks: Life is full of setbacks. It doesn't matter if you have been cut from the team or fired from your job. It doesn't matter if you've been demoted to the practice squad or belittled or devalued by someone close to you. And it doesn't even matter if you have had your season ended by injuries or you've received a negative medical diagnosis—setbacks happen. They are a part of everyone's life. But how you embrace and overcome setbacks is what truly shows your character. You have a God bigger than any setback, injury, or frustration. And God wants to use you right where you are to share His light with the world around you. "I can do all this through him who gives me strength" (Philippians 4:13).

Life was never promised to be easy, but you have a God who walks along the road with you. You never have to journey alone, and more importantly, God has a unique purpose He has created you to accomplish. God loves each person so intricately that He cares about every single moment of every day of our lives. You can't even say you own mother loves you that much! Trust God, and fight through your setbacks to accomplish the purpose God has for you.

DAY 8
HUMILITY WINS

Vernon Fox
NFL Veteran and Christian Speaker

By Beckie Lindsey

> Humble yourselves, therefore, under God's mighty hand,
> that he may lift you up in due time. Cast all your anxiety
> on him because he cares for you.
>
> —1 Peter 5:6–7

Do you ever notice how some people just seem to have a head
start in life? Veteran NFL player Vernon Fox is one of those
men most of us would consider fortunate. Being born in a
Christian home with loving parents and a natural ability to
play sports afforded him many opportunities at an early age.

By the time he was a junior in high school, he put all his
attention into football, which in turn gained him the attention
of several recruiting colleges.

"Every college I sent my highlight recruiting film to offered
me a full-ride scholarship," he said.

Vernon knew right away when he arrived at Fresno State it
was the school he wanted to attend. He excelled on and off the
field and was recognized as an Academic All-American. During
college he discovered what it meant to have his own faith in
God apart from being raised in a Christian home.

Only a few years down the road, his newfound faith in God would be put to the test when Vernon's entryway into the NFL was not what he expected. Having been successful all his life, he expected a million-dollar contract. He was projected to be a third or fourth-round draft pick in 2002. But he wasn't picked. As a young man of 23, he felt like a failure.

"For the first time, someone was telling me I wasn't good enough. It was very humbling. I had a lot of pride. My athletic success had tainted me. All that time I was pumping myself up, feeling like my abilities, talents, and skills caused me to achieve success. God showed me that wasn't why," he said.

Vernon went on to share how his perceived failure was used to learn reliance upon God. He felt overlooked, hopeless, and that his dreams of the NFL were impossible. It was at this point Vernon said there was a shift in his outlook. He was at a chapel service when the chaplain of the San Diego Chargers, Shawn Mitchell, said, "You have to work like it all depends on you and pray like it all depends on God."

From that moment on, he was on his face in humility before God each day. "I couldn't depend on anything else. It was a time of stripping where I disassociated myself from everything and everyone and focused on my goal of serving God. I knew if [the NFL] was going to happen, it would be led by God. I wanted to be everything He wanted me to be, and that meant cleaning up some areas of my life."

Within a matter of four months, Vernon went from being the last person signed on the San Diego Chargers to becoming a sixth string strong safety. He went on to make the final fifty-three-man roster, and in only his second game of the NFL, he earned a starting role. This time, he knew it was God's doing and not his own.

Have circumstances in your life brought you to a place of surrender in humility to God? Perhaps the Lord is speaking to you now.

Humble yourselves before the Lord, and he will lift you up.
—James 4:10

In the Huddle

Humility doesn't mean you put yourself down. To be humble, you don't need to neglect yourself. Truly humble people simply spend more time thinking about others than about themselves—meaning they are not self-preoccupied.

Humility is not thinking less of myself; it is thinking more of others.

Humility is not something God wants to "inflict" upon you.

God's desire is to lift you up. He doesn't want to humble you. He wants you to *be humble*. And there is a big difference. Allow that to sink in for a moment. "For those who exalt themselves will be humbled, and those who humble themselves will be exalted" (Matthew 23:12).

Humble people value God's truth over everything else, which may include risking relational harmony— and that can come off as not "nice."

Take Jesus for example. He gave up His divine privileges and took the humble position of a slave when He was born a human being. Then He humbled Himself in obedience to God when He died a criminal's death on a Cross (Philippians 2:7–8).

And yet, Jesus called religious leaders a "brood of vipers" (Matthew 12:34) and sons of the devil (John 8:44). He also called the crowd and even His own disciples an "unbelieving and perverse generation" (Matthew 17:17). But Jesus always humbly spoke the truth in love in order to build up and not tear down.

Cross the Goal Line

<u>Five Benefits to Humility:</u>

- God looks upon with favor and works through the humble: "'Has not my hand made all these things, and so they came into being?' declares the LORD. 'These are the ones I look on with favor: those who are humble and contrite in spirit, and who tremble at my word'" (Isaiah 66:2).
- Humility is key to gaining wisdom: "When pride comes, then comes disgrace, but with humility comes wisdom" (Proverbs 11:2).
- Humility prepares the heart for God's grace: "But he gives more grace. That is why Scripture says, 'God opposes the proud, but shows favor to the humble'" (James 4:6).
- God rewards the humble: "Humility is the fear of the LORD; its wages are riches and honor and life" (Proverbs 22:4).
- Christ dwells with the humble: "For this is what the high and exalted One says—he who lives forever, whose name is holy: 'I live in a high and holy place, but also with the one who is contrite and lowly in spirit, to revive the spirit of the lowly and to revive the heart of the contrite'" (Isaiah 57:15).

The opposite of humility is pride. And pride is a serious offense to God. It says, "I am great, and I don't need anyone's help, including God's." The angel Lucifer (aka Satan) was banished from heaven because of his pride. Like Vernon Fox, when we humbly allow the Lord to shine through our gifts and talents, we will not only score on the field of life but also in eternity. We must not be fooled into thinking humility means weakness or will lead to finishing last. God sees humility as a strength, and in heaven the last will be first and the first will be last (Matthew 20:16). In the end, humility wins.

> Humility is the foundation of all the other virtues hence, in the soul in which this virtue does not exist there cannot be any other virtue except in mere appearance.
>
> —St. Augustine

DAY 9
CALLING THE PLAYS

Jim Kelly
Hall of Fame Quarterback
Buffalo Bills

By Scott McCausey

But the Helper, the Holy Spirit, whom the Father will send in my name, he will teach you all things and bring to your remembrance all that I have said to you.

—John 14:26 ESV

The quarterback grasped the stick and scribed a big X in the dirt. "Okay guys, this X is me. Johnny, you line up to the right as this circle. You are going to run a fly pattern. Make sure Billy and Stan follow you. Andre, you are this square. You are going to run an out pattern. As soon as Johnny clears the right side I'll hit you about ten yards from the line of scrimmage. The rest of you guys block for me. Okay, on three, ready break!"

Communication in the huddle is a key to a successful offense. Typically, the players have studied their playbook and know the plays, but the skill of a quarterback's delivery in the huddle is as important as simply telling the group: "Flanker right, thirty-two-dive on one".

Jim Kelly not only excelled in the huddle, but he understands how people react to the message being delivered. "It's not always what you say, although that is important, it's how you say it," he emphasized. "You don't want to scare someone away; you need to know how to relate your message to them in a way that's comfortable."

Jim also shares the importance of understanding your audience. If you know you are chatting with someone who has a grumpy demeanor or defensive character trait, you can tailor the presentation of your message in a way they can relate. This doesn't mean you have to agree with your audience, but communicating in a way that is nonconfrontational can open a dialogue to effectively share your point of view. In the huddle, it calms nerves when teammates see their leader's control and hear a commanding voice. This is especially true in tense or high-pressure situations.

In the Huddle

Engaging in a debate or simply trying to share your point of view can be stressful. I've heard it said before that public speaking is one of people's greatest fears, but for some people, even speaking out in a small group can be intimidating. Sharing your heart can seem impossible. How do you cope with difficult conversations looming on the horizon? Do you put it off as long as possible? Do you excuse yourself from the chat or simply keep your mouth quiet if you know the topic is about to become controversial?

Cross the Goal Line

Having confidence to be bold is a key to effective communication. This allows our Christian witness to be seen and heard in a way that honors our Heavenly Father. "If you want to be a leader on the football field or to share the Bible, you have to know how to approach the conversation. Everyone is different, so relating to each personality is key," Jim noted. Delivering a message to a large group or ten other guys in a huddle takes courage and can be exemplified in our work place, home, and school. Here are some ideas to make this task more manageable.

- Practice and rehearse: Locking yourself in a closet is not going to help gain confidence. "Be strong and courageous. Do not be afraid or terrified because of them [enemy nations], for the LORD your God goes with you; he will never leave you nor forsake you" (Deuteronomy 31:6). Being bold begins with sharing your thoughts with friends and family inside your comfort zone. The disciples didn't begin challenging the religious leaders of the day without first asking questions and sharing ideas with Jesus. We build confidence when we talk through difficult topics with those we are close to. Gaining comfort in communication takes time.

- Listen: Communication is a two-way street. Being a good listener will do a couple things. It will convey to the person you are talking to you are willing to hear them. Next, it will advance the conversation by understanding the perspective of the person you are talking to.

- Know your audience: Understanding the personality of those you are talking to will help define how things will go. Strong willed individuals can be harder to reach with your ideas, so practicing patience will help. "Whoever is slow to anger is better than the mighty, and he who rules his spirit than he who takes a city" (Proverbs 16:32 ESV).

- Consider your target audience: Is it a group of kids, elderly, a church group, men, or women? Does your target audience know the love of Jesus Christ? This will help prepare the delivery of what you have to say.
- Know the points of view: Everyone has an opinion. In the midst of the huddle, the running back will probably want the ball, the receiver says throw the ball to him instead, and the coach desires his game plan to be followed. How does the quarterback discern the best course of action? Generally, the coach knows best. This is certainly the case in Scripture. "Thus says the LORD, your Redeemer, the Holy One of Israel: 'I am the LORD your God, who teaches you to profit, who leads you in the way you should go'" (Isaiah 48:17 ESV). Although several of points of view exist, remember God's Word during all discussions.
- Convey the love of Christ: Through it all, communicate the love of Jesus. Always keep this in mind, and no matter how the conversation goes, Jesus will win the day. "Let all that you do be done in love" (1 Corinthians 16:14 ESV).

Football is a sport where eleven players must be on the same page. If one player doesn't understand the play because it hasn't been communicated properly, he may run in the wrong direction, causing a fumble or missing a block leading to a sack.

"Getting Andre Reed to run a good route and not yelling at him if he runs a different route, this takes time. I'm not perfect, but I try to make sure people see God by my actions and how I talk to them," Jim said.

Talking to people is an art, and we need help. Allow the Holy Spirit to work in your life and prepare the way for victory.

When you want to deliver the right call to the appropriate audience, try to recall these steps and get the message out in the right fashion. Know what you want to say and how to communicate your message. If Jim did not know the plays in the huddle then his offense would have sputtered. He studied the playbook and knew what to say at the right time. You as a Christian need to study your playbook—the Word of God—and be confident when you deliver His message. Speak with love and compassion but also with authority because you know deep down how the play will eventually come to pass. Speak in love.

DAY 10
NEVER GIVE UP

DeAndre Hopkins
Pro-Bowl Wide Receiver
Houston Texans

By Del Duduit

And let us not grow weary of doing good, for in due season
we will reap, if we do not give up.
—Galatians 6:9 ESV

DeAndre Hopkins has seen his share of personal challenges.

He never knew his father, who died in a car accident when
he was just a few months old.

His mother was seriously injured when he was ten. She lost
her sight in one eye and almost went blind in the other. His
uncle was killed, and a cousin tried to commit suicide.

In 2012, DeAndre suffered a concussion when he was
involved in a car accident on his way to catch the team bus for
Clemson University's appearance in the Orange Bowl.

"My whole life was tough growing up," he said. "We all have
obstacles to overcome. It seemed for me, growing up in Section
8 housing as a young black man was really tough. I'm not complaining, but that's just how life was for me then."

But his mother made sure he was raised in church where he
learned to lean on God and avoid resentment about his situation.

"My faith is a big, big thing for me," he said. "It is a major part of my life, and my mom made sure I knew about God."

Today, she still sends him a prayer before each game, and he credits his success to her determination.

"She raised us in tough times, held down two jobs, and I watched her faith grow stronger and stronger," he said. "She showed me the importance of hard work and to trust in the man upstairs. I never forgot that."

He is open and transparent about his spirituality, to the point he held a public baptism after practice at Clemson one day in 2012. He said he wanted to let his peers and teammates know his life was dedicated to Jesus Christ.

DeAndre worked his way to earn a first-round draft pick in 2013. He has been named first-team All-Pro and made two Pro-Bowl appearances. In 2017, he was the NFL touchdown leader for receivers.

He could have decided at a younger age to go in a different direction and develop a hostility toward the church and God. But his mother took him to worship services and taught him to honor his heavenly Father.

"No matter how hard life can get, you can never give up," he said. "Just work hard, live right, and have faith in the Lord."

> But you, take courage! Do not let your hands be weak, for your work shall be rewarded.
>
> —2 Chronicles 15:7 ESV

In the Huddle

Has life come down hard on you? Perhaps you lost your job or you are in over your head in debt with no immediate way out.

Maybe you received some disturbing news from your doctor or lost someone close to you. The one person you vowed to spend your life with told you she wants out. Or maybe you have had a string of events that have collectively annoyed you and brought you down. You don't see God anywhere, and you pray to no avail. Have you been there? What do you do in these times?

Cross the Goal Line

When life sacks you in the backfield for a big loss, don't send in the punting team yet. Draw up a game plan and a strategy to put yourself into scoring position. You can make a big play to give yourself better field position and make it possible to score on the next opportunity. But success doesn't just happen. You must develop a strong mindset and demonstrate faith in the Lord when times are tough. Don't give up. Instead, put your game face on, grind your teeth, and be prepared to plow through the struggle. There are ways to strengthen your resolve when life gets tough to handle. Here are some tips to give you a faithful attitude of determination:

- Listen more in prayer: Many people are in a habit of asking for things when they pray. However, try to begin with thanks, and praise Him first. A few requests are okay, but be sure to plead for His direction and be still. God will speak to you if you can withstand the quietness of the moment. "If you will diligently listen to the voice of the LORD your God, and do that which is right in his eyes, and give ear to his commandments and keep all his statutes, I will put none of the diseases on you that I put on the Egyptians, for I am the LORD, your healer" (Exodus 15:26 ESV).

- Keep your appointments: God likes to hear from you. If you want to be able to get through difficult situations, you must be consistent in your devotion time with the Master. If you set aside a certain time of the day, do your best to stay on schedule. You don't miss the designated time you have set with a doctor or a mechanic, so be sure to show up for your time alone with God, and do this daily. If this means you must adjust your sleep pattern and get up earlier, then do so. This will bring you closer to the Lord. "But when you pray, go into your room and shut the door and pray to your Father who is in secret. And your Father who sees in secret will reward you" (Matthew 6:6 ESV).

- Accept suffering as God's way to prepare you to help others: Tough experiences will equip you to handle struggles and train you to counsel others who go through trials in life. If you depend on God for His plan, your faith will grow stronger, and you will develop an attitude of total trust in the Savior. Lean on the Lord and follow His lead. "Blessed be the God and Father of our Lord Jesus Christ, the Father of mercies and God of all comfort, who comforts us in all our affliction, so that we may be able to comfort those who are in any affliction, with the comfort with which we ourselves are comforted by God" (2 Corinthians 1:3–4 ESV).

- Praise God in the storm: When you glorify the Father with a genuine heart through difficult situations, you will become stronger. Praising God may not remove the issues that trouble you, but you will deal with them in a better state of mind. When you lift your hands in praise, your loved one won't come back to life, but God will give you encouragement to face another day. When you honor the Father, you may not get your job back, but you will have peace in the time of trouble. Trust the Lord to send someone special into your life or to receive a phone call from a job recruiter. Praise Him through it all. "Fear not, for I am with you; be not dismayed, for I am your God; I will strengthen you, I will help you, I will uphold you with my righteous right hand" (Isaiah 41:10 ESV).

DeAndre could have tossed in the towel and quit as a teenager. But instead, he stayed in church, worked hard, and practiced his faith, and today, he is a wonderful role model for young kids. When the going gets tough, rely on the Lord, and let Him fight your battles for you. Hold on for the ride of your life, and never give up.

DAY 11
NO COMPROMISE

Mark Sanchez
Quarterback
Chicago Bears

By Ryan Farr

So he told her everything. "No razor has ever been used on my head," he said, "because I have been a Nazirite dedicated to God from my mother's womb. If my head were shaved, my strength would leave me, and I would become as weak as any other man."

—Judges 16:17

Mark Sanchez knows what it means to be successful on the gridiron. As an accomplished quarterback who was an All-Pac 10 selection and a fifth-overall NFL Draft pick, he realizes cutting corners is never the way to go. A quarterback like Mark knows that to be the starter at a college like the University of South Carolina and an NFL franchise like the Philadelphia Eagles and New York Jets takes discipline. It means long hours of drills with teammates, coaches, and, occasionally, on his own. It means a tight lifting regime and a strict diet that keep him in top shape. And there are times when, despite the commitment, things don't pan out the way you want.

"It would be easy to let the worries of your job get to you," he said. "Maybe there's a time where I'm not playing or not in the situation I had planned for." So, what does Mark do when facing these times of self-doubt? He considers the ways God has blessed him. "I think, 'Man, thank You, Lord,'" he added. "Thank You for helping me or putting people in my life or taking me down a certain path."

And to what does Mark credit his ability to keep his head up even in the toughest of times? For starters, it was a great family upbringing that taught him never to compromise his faith. "It started with my mom," Mark said. "When I was young she took me to Vacation Bible School and church and after-school day care with a faith-based curriculum." What was exemplified to him as a child has shown itself in the man and teammate he's become.

With the lifestyle of an NFL quarterback, Mark faces many temptations on a daily basis. So how has he been able to keep from compromising his walk with Christ in the midst of it all? He recalls a Bible study, *The Samson Syndrome*: "The 'Samson syndrome' is where you can get caught up in yourself and you make a series of compromises," he said. "Soon you are hanging with the wrong crew or doing the wrong things—compromising here and there—soon you don't recognize yourself." Through accountability with family and teammates, Mark has been committed to walking in step with God's plan for his life.

"My faith keeps my life in perspective," he said. "My faith is everything to me."

In the Huddle

Hearing about Mark Sanchez's faith and his commitment to make no compromises is inspiring. But it's harder than it may seem. We live in a world that has starkly different values from those we see in God's Word. You may not be an NFL quarterback fighting off the bad habits of celebrity life, but all of us have struggles. In what ways are you tempted to compromise your faith in God, and what has He called you to do in your life? How can you find accountability as you resist that temptation?

Cross the Goal Line

As you consider these questions, it is important to recognize when you are being put in a situation that may compromise what God has called you to do. In those times, it is important to consider the following.

- Walk humbly: If you get a chance, read the story of Samson in Judges 16. Samson's self-centered demeanor began to rely more on himself than God for direction. There couldn't be a more dangerous attitude. "Be completely humble and gentle; be patient, bearing with one another in love" (Ephesians 4:2).
- Stay in the game: Many of the things you will forego in life in exchange for living according to God's will may seem like big sacrifices. In the end, God has a larger plan that will ultimately lead you to where He wants you to go. "Where there is no guidance, a people falls, but in an abundance of counselors there is safety" (Proverbs 11:14 ESV).
- Give no footholds: Samson kept the secret of his strength his entire life . . . but one moment of weakness ended up costing him everything. Keep God the center of all your decisions, even the small and seemingly insignificant ones of everyday life. God calls us to honor Him with every area of our lives.

- Pray with confidence: Never underestimate the power of going right to God in prayer, asking Him to give you the wisdom to discern His will. "This is the confidence we have in approaching God: that if we ask anything according to his will, he hears us" (1 John 5:14).
- Seek accountability: There is nothing like solid, God-honoring partnership and accountability when facing trials or temptations. Seek out others who can provide godly counsel and tough love when needed.

Life is not an easy road. Remaining committed to God will undoubtedly mean making choices that seem as though you are sacrificing relationships and what you perceive as good experiences. But rest assured, the Lord has not given us His Word to restrict us but rather to allow us to live in freedom from the world and its ways. As you continue to be a person who walks with Christ and doesn't make compromises, you will see Him transform your heart in ways you couldn't have imagined.

DAY 12
YOU CAN ALWAYS MAKE A COMEBACK

Chad Pennington
Quarterback
New York Jets

By Del Duduit

If we confess our sins, he is faithful and just to forgive us our sins and to cleanse us from all unrighteousness.
—1 John 1:9 ESV

Chad Pennington knows a little something about how to make a return in style.

The Marshall University product won the NFL Comeback Player of the Year (CPOTY) two times, which is rare for any athlete.

In 2005, he underwent two surgeries for a torn rotator cuff. The next year, he led the New York Jets to a 10–6 regular season mark, posted 3,352 yards in the air, and took the team to the playoffs. New York's previous record was 4–12. Chad earned his first CPOTY award for his performance.

"That felt good to be recognized for all the hard work and dedication I put in to come back," he said. "That meant a lot."

But the next season did not start well for him. He suffered an ankle injury, which affected his capabilities on the field. He was eventually benched midway, but then he saw action later in the year. Prior to the start of the 2008 season, New York released him when they signed veteran signal caller Brett Favre.

He then joined the Miami Dolphins where he had a spectacular year. He completed a league-leading 67.4 completion percentage, which broke Miami's previous single-season record holder Dan Marino in 1984. He finished the year with a passer rating of 97.4 percent and led the Dolphins to an 11–5 record. He threw for more than 3,500 yards and tied for second in the MVP race, behind winner Peyton Manning.

Chad's motivated performance earned him his second CPOTY award in 2008. He showed the sports world it is possible to come back from difficult situations and make your mark. He experienced wins and losses along with injuries. But he always kept the right perspective.

"I don't think the appreciation level ever changes. You just have to understand that there's always going to be highs and lows," he said. "And it's always to the extreme, because the middle of the road doesn't sail, and it's not exciting. The extremes—that's what's exciting, and that is what everybody leans on."

> For the righteous falls seven times and rises again, but the wicked stumble in times of calamity.
>
> —Proverbs 24:16 ESV

Huddle Up

Have you ever been injured as a follower of Jesus Christ? Was there a time when a person you trusted betrayed you or told lies about you to other people? Perhaps you were wronged by a leader in your church, or maybe you are the one who erred. No matter what happened or who did it, you may have drifted in your spiritual walk with the Lord.

Cross the Goal Line

People stumble and make mistakes that can lead to an emotional and spiritual injury. Chad came back from a serious shoulder injury to lead his team to the playoffs. The next year, several factors played a role in his trip to the bench. But he didn't give up. He felt betrayed when he was cut from the Jets, but he kept his head held high and worked harder than ever. He could have retired or complained to the media, but he chose the high road.

When fellow Christians hurt you, don't give up or allow the devil to persuade you to pull away from your loved ones or church family. Be on guard for the signs you are drifting further from the Lord than you realize. Keep an eye out for red flags, like the ones in the following list, and let them serve as your two-minute warning to get back into the game before it ends in defeat:

- You cut back or stop reading the Bible: This is the first sign you are about to backslide. When you don't make the Word of God a priority each day, you will miss out on much needed fellowship with Christ along with any important messages He may have for you.
- Your prayer life goes astray: When you don't talk to God, you place yourself in a dangerous position. How would you feel if your child gave you the silent treatment for days? You know something is wrong but cannot force the issue. God is patient and will forgive you. He died for your sins and has promised you eternal life. Daily conversations with Him must be part of your routine in order to maintain a close relationship.

- You stop attending church: This is a public sign you have turned your back on the Lord, but have you separated yourself from the church or from the actions of those who have hurt you? You cannot protest your salvation based on what others may have done. If you feel you cannot go back to your church, find another and keep your reasons to yourself. Never run anyone else down to justify your actions.
- You judge others: Do not concern yourself with people you believe get away with poor choices and evil behavior. God is in control, and His justice will reign. When evil leads others to prosperity, it is His job to correct the situation and not yours. Don't use the wicked actions of others to justify your sin.
- You ignore what you know is right: When you act out of spite with full awareness of the potential consequences, you walk a very thin line. Your decisions can affect your loved ones. Maybe your kids love to go to Sunday school, yet you have a grudge against someone in the church and decide to keep them home. Do what is best for them, and put your own desires on the back burner.

If you have been harmed or damaged by others, be aware of how you respond. If you have experienced any of the red flags just mentioned, take inventory immediately. God will allow you to make a comeback, but you have to make the call—no one can make it for you. Don't concentrate on what others have done. Turn your situation over to Christ, and let Him deal with it while you focus on your relationship with Him. When you start to feel yourself fall away, take action and seek the Lord's forgiveness. "I will give them a heart to know that I am the LORD, and they shall be my people and I will be their God, for they shall return to me with their whole heart" (Jeremiah 24:7 ESV). Make the comeback.

DAY 13
TAKE ADVANTAGE OF OPPORTUNITIES

Kurt Warner
Hall of Fame Quarterback
Arizona Cardinals

By Del Duduit

Preaching the kingdom of God, and teaching those things which concern the Lord Jesus Christ, with all confidence, no man forbidding him.

—Acts 28:31 KJV

Over the years, a few professional athletes have made some audacious statements. Some use them to try to intimidate their opponents while others blather them due to a cocky attitude.

Let's look back at three audacious statements I like:

In 1963, Muhammad Ali (then known as Cassius Clay) joked and rhymed his way to a fearless prediction about his heavyweight fight with Henry Cooper when he said, "This is no jive; Cooper shall go down in five." The referee stopped the fight in the fifth round because Cooper's eye was swollen shut.

In 1969 just before Super Bowl III, when it was predicted the New York Jets had little chance of beating the highly favored Baltimore Colts, Jets quarterback Joe Namath famously said, "Hey, I got news for you. We're going to win Sunday, I'll guarantee you." New York won the game 16–7 over the Colts.

And who can forget when Boston Celtics legend Larry Bird told everyone in the locker room he would win the inaugural three-point shootout during the 1986 NBA All-Star Weekend? The future Hall of Famer walked into the locker room and sized up his competition. "Which one of you guys is going to finish second?" he asked. Bird won hands down and even connected on eleven straight three-pointers in the final round.

But the one that takes the cake is what Kurt Warner did on national television after his Arizona Cardinals won the NFC Championship game in 2009 to advance to the Super Bowl.

During the post-game interview, live on TV with Terry Bradshaw, he thanked and praised his Savior Jesus Christ.

And prior to that, in 2000, after his St. Louis Rams won Super Bowl XXXIV, Warner did the same thing. He acknowledged Christ to millions who watched the celebration.

"I think one of the greatest moves I ever made was when I professed Jesus on the podium after I won the Super Bowl," he said. "Because now, everyone knows about my faith."

His boldness brought about accountability as a Christian. Now, he had to be the example in front of the audience.

"When I did that and thanked Jesus, it pushed me to be more accountable with my faith and turned out to be the greatest blessing I've enjoyed," he added. "Everyone knows that I'm a Christian, and I love that."

And for me, that utterance may be given unto me, that I may open my mouth boldly, to make known the mystery of the gospel.

—Ephesians 6:19 KJV

In the Huddle

You might find yourself in a situation where you have the opportunity to let those around you know you are a follower of Christ. You might be given a chance to speak in public or be called on at work to explain why you have been successful. These moments can intimidate you but also might not happen too often. What will you do if given a platform to proclaim the Master?

Cross the Goal Line

You want to be careful not to turn people off, but at the same time, capitalize on any opportunity you get to confess your Savior. Tell others in love about the mighty God you serve. Be brief but excited to let others know you follow Jesus Christ. Here are some tips to help you become bold in in sharing your faith:

- Be confident: Kurt did not back away from the microphone. He thanked Jesus Christ with courage and humility. How did the crowd respond? His fans went crazy. If you are presented with a similar situation (hopefully you will win a Super Bowl), seize the moment. After all, Christ died for you. In return, you can at least thank Him in public.
- Pray: You can thank God in front of people before lunch or dinner. This doesn't have to be a hell-fire-and-brimstone prayer or even all that long, but you should make it subtle and sincere. When people see you bow your head in prayer, they might be encouraged to do the same. "For there is one God, and one mediator between God and men, the man Christ Jesus" (1 Timothy 2:5 KJV).

- Use social media: Let your followers on social media know where you stand, but don't drive them away. Post an occasional sentence of inspiration with a Scripture verse attached. You don't have to do this all the time, just mix it in with a picture of your puppy or granddaughter. Put a line in your profile that tells everyone you love the Lord. You might even add your favorite Bible verse. For example, Aaron Judge's Twitter profile describes him the following way: "Christian. Faith, Family, then Baseball." When your friends and followers know where you stand, you will become more accountable in your Christian journey. "And blessed be his glorious name for ever: and let the whole earth be filled with his glory; Amen, and Amen" (Psalm 72:19 KJV).
- Testify in church: Just a few simple words of thanks will suffice. A personal story will also let those around you know you are grateful for God's mercy. "Be not thou therefore ashamed of the testimony of our Lord, nor of me his prisoner: but be thou partaker of the afflictions of the gospel according to the power of God" (2 Timothy 1:8 KJV).
- Lead a Bible study: Gather a group of friends and open your home for a time of devotion once a week or perhaps monthly. Use this time to share your personal testimony, and encourage others to share their stories too. Present the plan of salvation at each meeting and give attendees an invitation to pray and ask Jesus into their hearts.

The odds are high you will never be given a microphone to use in front of millions of viewers after you have won the Super Bowl. Kurt received that opportunity and made the most of it by thanking Jesus Christ. You don't have to be on stage to proclaim your love and devotion to the Savior, but be ready at all times to make the call.

DAY 14
DON'T BE AFRAID TO SPEAK OUT

Tom Lamphere
Chaplain
Minnesota Vikings

By Del Duduit

For we wrestle not against flesh and blood, but against principalities, against powers, against the rulers of the darkness of this world, against spiritual wickedness in high places.

—Ephesians 6:12 KJV

In more than twenty-five years as chaplain for the Minnesota Vikings, Tom Lamphere has seen it all.

He has witnessed the good along with the bad. The way he lives his life in front of the team is his best testimony and witness for the Lord.

One of the struggles many Christian players face is media bias or a lack of true understanding from the press. If an athlete thanks the Lord or gives praise to God at a post-game interview, most of the time that segment does not air or make the print edition.

"They get a little upset because they will do the interview, talk from the heart, then all the spiritual stuff gets clipped out," Tom said. "I warn them that it's going to happen and not to let it bother them, but it does."

Several professional athletes have a strong testimony, and examples include Tim Tebow, Benjamin Watson, Nick Foles, and Tony Dungy. Many times their public testimonies also do not make the reel.

"I don't think the media knows how to handle it," Tom said. "I don't believe it's a bias toward a certain player. I honestly think they just don't know how to deal with it, so they ignore it, or they think the people don't want to hear it."

But he knows fans want to hear about what drives an athlete. "They absolutely want to be exposed to their faith," he said. "When Kurt Warner thanked Jesus on national television after they won the Super Bowl, the place went crazy. The response from the crowd after he acknowledged Jesus was amazing."

The harvest is plentiful, but the workers are few, he added.

"When Jesus was talking with His apostles, he told them to look at all the people and said the people are out there and ready," he said. "The problem isn't the harvest—the problem is we don't have enough harvesters."

He says players who follow Christ need to continue to spread the gospel any way they can. If a microphone is shoved in their faces after a game, players should tell all who listen about the goodness of the Lord.

"Most of the time the attention goes to those who are doing it all wrong," Tom said. "And there are a bunch of kids out there watching. Christian players are the ones our youth need to hear from because they are the ones who make the right decisions in all aspects of life—community, church, and personal."

These things I have spoken unto you, that in me ye might have peace. In the world ye shall have tribulation; but be of good cheer; I have overcome the world.
—John 16:33 KJV

Huddle Up

You may never be interviewed on national television like many of the players in the NFL, but you can still have a tremendous impact on those around you. When you stand up for your beliefs, what actions do you take? Have you had opportunities to speak up for the Savior and neglected to follow through? Have you missed chances to brag on the Lord? When you tell others about your accomplishments, do you give glory to God? If not, the time is here to make a change and shine the light on Christ where the attention belongs.

Cross the Goal Line

Maybe you let a moment slip by when you could have given praise to God. You want to demonstrate a grateful heart, but at the same time you don't want to come across as overbearing to others. But there are ways to magnify the name of the Lord in such a way to let everyone around you know where you stand. Here are some suggestions:

- Live the life: You must walk the walk if you intend to establish credibility as a Christian. This means you must have a desire to attend church on a regular basis and not cut out when it's inconvenient. Do good in the sight of those around you, and live a righteous life at home too. If you exhibit behavior in your home that could compromise your testimony, stop it. What you do in private says a lot about your character. "Boast not thyself of to morrow; for thou knowest not what a day may bring forth" (Proverbs 27:1 KJV).

- Understand your role: If you are a father, your children watch every move you make even when you don't realize it. If you have a high-stress job, your coworkers will watch to see how you handle the pressure. Your influence is broader than you may think.
- Become involved: Be active not only in your church but also in local community organizations. Find a group with a cause near and dear to your heart and jump in. Perhaps you are passionate about upholding the sanctity of life. Find your local pro-life chapter and ask how to become involved. If you have a desire to help people in need, check out the local Red Cross or other civic organization. Sign up with Big Brothers Big Sisters. Once you join, stay dedicated and be trustworthy. "As every man hath received the gift, even so minister the same one to another, as good stewards of the manifold grace of God" (1 Peter 4:10 KJV).
- Run for office: Christian leaders are needed at every level. This will also give you a platform to let everyone know about your moral obligations and your character. Our nation needs people of strong faith to lead the charge.
- Establish a ministry: This does not have to be groundbreaking, but it could grow into something big. Perhaps you could start a Bible study or launch a writing ministry. There are many ways you can influence others who need to hear about the gospel. Use your talents to spread the gospel.

These are just a few of many ways you can spread the gospel of Christ to your community. There is never a wrong time to start, but there is danger in procrastination. The longer you sit back and let others take action, the more the devil will tell you to let them do the work. Tom said the harvest is ready, but there are not enough workers. The application has already been filled out, and the job is yours. All you have to do is report to work and get busy for God. "Take therefore no thought for the morrow; for the morrow shall take thought for the things of itself. Sufficient unto the day is the evil thereof" (Matthew 6:34 KJV).

DAY 15
GOD CAN BRING YOU THROUGH
YOUR VALLEY

Morgan Cox
Pro-Bowl Long-Snapper and
Super Bowl Champion
Baltimore Ravens

By Del Duduit

Therefore, my beloved brothers, be steadfast, immovable,
always abounding in the work of the Lord, knowing that
in the Lord your labor is not in vain.

—1 Corinthians 15:58 ESV

Morgan Cox stays under the radar, even though he is a two-time Pro-Bowl long-snapper and Super Bowl winner with the Baltimore Ravens.

The media rarely interviews him, unless he makes a mistake. His role is vital to the team, but he does not see his name in headlines or make the highlight reel on ESPN.

This is how he prefers life to be for him.

"I don't like all the attention some of the guys get, so it's perfect for me. I love my job, and I love being around all these guys in the locker rom," he said.

He has come back from two ACL injuries to do his job, which is to fire the ball back to a kicker or punter. When he experienced these times of discouragement, Morgan leaned on Christ to get him through some difficult days.

"I've had my share of ups and downs, just like anyone in this league or in life in general," he said. "That is why I try to stay grounded, and that's when my faith helps me stay strong."

When the two injuries put his career in doubt, Morgan had a peace through Christ that got him through each day.

"Playing in the NFL was never something I thought would be possible," he said. "But it goes to show if you put your trust in the Lord, He will lead you to wonderful places."

Morgan knows he can come back from anything if he stays close to the Master and has the support of his loved ones.

"They keep me grounded," he said. "My faith and my family are the reason I do what I do. It's been an amazing journey."

> For I know the plans I have for you, declares the LORD, plans for welfare and not for evil, to give you a future and a hope.
>
> —Jeremiah 29:11 ESV

In the Huddle

Has an injury put you in the dumps? You may suffer from a physical injury like Morgan did, or you may suffer an emotional injury at the expense of a friend, colleague, or fellow church member. Perhaps someone told a lie about you or hurt your loved ones. These kinds of betrayals are tough to come back from, in particular when they come from those you never suspected. These happen, but you must know there is a way to find victory and bounce back.

Cross the Goal Line

When you take a blow to your spiritual side, you must view Christ as your personal trainer and emotional healer. A good athlete recovers from an injury if he follows orders from his doctor and visits his physical therapist when recommended. When the time is right, he will make his comeback on the field of play. An injured child of God must follow similar steps. The first course of action is to set up an appointment with the Divine Physician. Here are some suggestions on how to heal quickly and get back in the game:

- Forgive the one who caused the pain: This is the hardest step, which is why it needs to happen first. Maybe the person who wronged you did not ask to be forgiven—do it anyway. Once you pass this obstacle, the healing can begin. "For if you forgive others their trespasses, your heavenly Father will also forgive you" (Matthew 6:14 ESV).
- Clean the wound: This is an essential part of the recuperation. If you have a physical wound, you sterilize it. The same goes for scars of the heart. This can be a painful process, but you must strive to purge the bitterness and resentment you may harbor. "If we confess our sins, he is faithful and just to forgive us our sins and to cleanse us from all unrighteousness" (1 John 1:9 ESV). When you seethe with anger and allow hostility to fester and grow, you will never mend. But when you cleanse your wound with forgiveness that only comes with help from the Father above, you will begin the road to a complete recovery.
- Apply protection: After you purify the wound, you must dress it with bandages, ointment, or other medicine to protect it from further infection. The same is true for

Christians. The best way to protect the wound is to use a spiritual balm, one that can be found through prayer and study of the Word of God. Time is a friend. Allow the process to work. "You are a hiding place for me; you preserve me from trouble; you surround me with shouts of deliverance." (Psalm 32:7 ESV).

- Observe and wait: For any cut or scrape, make sure you don't put the injury at risk. Don't repeat the action that brought on the affliction. If you touched a hot stove, don't do it again. If you were cut when you used a sharp knife, then learn how to use the utensil the correct way. The same goes for wounds of the spirit. If a person lies about you, then stay out of that person's circle, if possible. Watch for the warning signs and step back when you see them, but make sure you observe them with an open mind and heart. Listen to the instructions of the Lord. The devil—who caused this pain—would love to reopen the wound. Don't give him the opportunity. "Be sober-minded; be watchful. Your adversary the devil prowls around like a roaring lion, seeking someone to devour. Resist him, firm in your faith, knowing that the same kinds of suffering are being experienced by your brotherhood throughout the world" (1 Peter 5:8–9 ESV).

- Get back in the game: You were hurt for a reason. The forces of evil want to destroy you and will stop at nothing to accomplish their goals. Once you have recovered from your injury, you must get back out on the field. Stay in church and attend Sunday school or a Bible study. Become stronger in the Lord. When Morgan came back from his knee injuries, he wore braces for support and exercised his muscles. He doesn't want to go through that pain again. You must have the same goal. Become stronger in the Word. Establish times for your devotions on a regular basis. Memorize Scripture, and use it as a tool to boost your path to full recovery. "You do not have, because you do not ask" (James 4:2 ESV).

Morgan had doubts about his future career when he was injured, but he came back and loved his job. He returned stronger and better than ever. You too can also be renewed in your journey with Christ. Absorb the blow and do what is needed to get back on the field of play and win souls for the kingdom.

DAY 16
REASON TO SING

Ben Utecht
Super Bowl Champion Tight End
Indianapolis Colts

By Del Duduit

The LORD will keep you from all harm—he will watch over your life; the LORD will watch over your coming and going both now and forevermore.

—Psalm 121:7–8

Ben Utecht's stellar career in the NFL was cut short due to head injuries.

The talented tight end from Minnesota won a Super Bowl with the Indianapolis Colts. At six foot six and 245 pounds, he was a big target for quarterback Peyton Manning.

But over his career, he suffered at least five known concussions and experienced loss of memory by the age of thirty.

In 2014, he recorded a song titled "You Will Always Be My Girls," which he dedicated to his wife and daughters in the event his brain injuries ever prevent him from knowing who they are in the future.

Ultimately, Ben was placed on the injured reserve list, and he hung up his cleats. Music was always his passion and became his second career. After all, it was his first love in high school and college.

He recorded several albums, which include a Christmas album nominated for a Dove Award in 2012.

"I love music so much," he said. "I never prayed for success in music, but the Lord knew it was a passion of mine. My prayer was always, 'If it's something You want me to do, then bring the right people into my life.'"

This is exactly what God did. After he sang at a youth event in Indiana, Grammy Award-winning recording artist Sandi Patty, who was in the audience, approached him and said she was impressed by his performance. She introduced him to fellow gospel music powerhouses Bill and Gloria Gaither, and soon Ben cut his first album.

"If I had not gone to the Colts, I would never have sung at that rally and never met the people I did," he said. "God's timing and plan is amazing."

Today, he draws from his head injury experiences to talk to athletes, coaches, and parents about the dangers of concussions. He is a national spokesperson for the American Academy of Neurology and the American Brain Foundation. But he is also a speaker, author, singer, and a leader on Christ's playing field.

"I'm here because the Lord has plans for me," he said. "I love what I do for Jesus. I love to sing and speak in front of people and tell them how good God is to me."

Whatever you do, work at it with all your heart, as working for the Lord, not for human masters, since you know that you will receive an inheritance from the Lord as a reward. It is the Lord Christ you are serving.

—Colossians 3:23–24

In the Huddle

Have your plans changed? Did you have big dreams about your future that have never come true? Maybe your aspirations were to make it big on Broadway but instead you work an office job from nine to five. Or you may have wanted to be a famous author but you are on the sales team. Perhaps you wanted to be a coach and win the big game but you had to take a blue-collar shift job. Don't let Satan make you feel like a failure. The Lord may be preparing you for what He has in store for you. God put the perfect steps in order for Ben to meet Sandi Patty. And his big break may never have happened if he had not played professional football. All the head injuries, although tragic at the time, were part of God's perfect plan for him to help others who have faced similar circumstances and to bring awareness to the need for better safety protocols and equipment for professional athletes.

Cross the Goal Line

You can be what God wants you to be, but you must show patience. He is not on your schedule. It is human nature to question Christ, but to understand takes faith. The Lord turned Ben's dream to sing into a reality. What is your passion? What fire do you possess within that no one knows about? Are you willing to do whatever the Lord wants you to do? This may not always be easy, but He expects us to do His will and trust His plan for His glory. While you persevere through the anticipation for God to reveal His blueprint for your life, remember to do the following:

- Spend time in prayer: In the darkness of night, pour your heart out to the Lord, and He will listen. He knows what you want, but He asks you to trust Him. His answer may take a long time, but He will make the right call. God's timing is always perfect, but sometimes this is hard to see when you have waited for so long.

- Praise God through it all: You might be in a dead-end job, but give glory to the Lord anyway. *What?* That's right. Thank Him for the career you have now that helps you to pay the bills to meet your needs. He may use this to prepare you for a bigger adventure down the road, so lift your hands to honor Him. "As for me, I will always have hope; I will praise you more and more" (Psalm 71:14).

- Get ready: Expect God's blessings to happen. Prepare for the big day. A great example of this is found in 1 Corinthians 9:24–27 where Scripture tells about a race: "Do you not know that in a race all the runners run, but only one gets the prize? Run in such a way as to get the prize. Everyone who competes in the games goes into strict training. They do it to get a crown that will not last, but we do it to get a crown that will last forever. Therefore I do not run like someone running aimlessly; I do not fight like a boxer beating the air. No, I strike a blow to my body and make it my slave so that after I have preached to others, I myself will not be disqualified for the prize." Put yourself in a position to win the race. If you want to be a teacher, work hard in college and earn your degree. If you have a job now and want to become a lawyer, then take the first step and go to law school to prepare yourself.

- Keep the right attitude: Don't put your own selfish needs in front of God's plans. Ben's original passion was music, but he first played football. In whatever situation God places you, make the most of it and focus on being content.

"I know what it is to be in need, and I know what it is to have plenty. I have learned the secret of being content in any and every situation, whether well fed or hungry, whether living in plenty or in want. I can do all this through him who gives me strength" (Philippians 4:12–13).

- Press toward the goal: The point here is to keep moving. Take every opportunity to grow and learn. Listen for the coach to call your name and to give you the play He designed for you. When He does, look back and see how God used all the things you have gone through to groom you for this moment.

Ben showed patience and endured some serious physical injuries along the way. But God used him for His glory and has given him the desires of his heart. Be sure to have a song in your mouth at all times, and trust God to get you to the goal line.

DAY 17
TOUCHDOWN REMINDERS

Frank Murphy
Receiver
Tampa Bay Buccaneers

By Scott McCausey

The heart of man plans his way, but the LORD establishes his steps.

—Proverbs 16:9 ESV

Electricity filled Raymond James Stadium in anticipation of the Coach Jon Gruden-era in Tampa Bay. The Bucs finished 9–7 in 2001 but were routed in the wild card game by the Philadelphia Eagles, prompting the dismissal of Coach Tony Dungy. The Miami Dolphins came to town for this preseason battle and expectations were high.

The kickoff landed in the arms of second year player Frank Murphy, who cruised to his right and turned on the afterburners. His 4.22-second, 40-yard dash speed was in full display as he crossed the goal line 95 yards later. Over 60,000 fans screamed, and a national ESPN audience was thrilled with the start of the season, but none more than Frank.

"It's a reward God has for you even when you are trying to find the right path. A lot of people might say, 'This can't happen to me.' But when you're searching for the right path, God will show it to you through success reminders," he said.

Frank exhibits an understanding of God's plan through healthy Christian living. Yet his path to the NFL wasn't always one he envisioned. His struggle with high school scholastics forced him to play community college football, a challenge he embraced to the tune of not only attaining a 3.2 grade point average but also being named the National Junior College Athletic Association National Player of the Year in 1997 for Garden City Community College. He then transferred to Kansas State to start at running back before being drafted by the Bears and picked up the Buccaneers.

In the Huddle

Traveling the path dedicated to Jesus can be difficult and filled with unexpected U-turns. How do you know you're on the right one? Where does the path begin, and what does it look like? Frank trusted the skills God gifted him with, never allowing the world to keep him down. If the road to Jesus required a detour to fix imperfections, he took the alternate route.

Cross the Goal Line

Taking the road less traveled can be bumpy. There will also be a cost associated. The path might hurt and force us to abandon what looks good or feels right. It might take longer and require us to have patience. But God will sprinkle victories so we know the path is correct. Here's some helpful reminders when you struggle to understand God's path for you.

- Focus on the goal: A constant eye on the prize will put into perspective the path you are on. For example, God may reveal a job in another city to best utilize your gifts. He may unveil a college track you want to follow at a university that might be a few hundred miles away. God may even introduce you to a new circle of friends to encourage you. "You make known to me the path of life; in your presence there is fullness of joy; at your right hand are pleasures forevermore" (Psalm 16:11 ESV). God will reveal your path but keep watch to know you're on it.

- Take it for the team: A key block that leads to a touchdown is not glamorous, but without it, the team will suffer. You may have to provide that block for others to break free. Your job as ambassador for Jesus may not be popular, but Christianity isn't a popularity contest. It's a kingdom quest to introduce people to a better way of life. "As you come to him, a living stone rejected by men but in the sight of God chosen and precious, you yourselves like living stones are being built up as a spiritual house, to be a holy priesthood, to offer spiritual sacrifices acceptable to God through Jesus Christ" (1 Peter 2:4–5 ESV).

- Don't take the long way around: The shortest distance between two points is a straight line. However, we don't always stay on track. Temptations sidetrack goals and distract from the prize. Stay close to the Lord to avoid a path of destruction. Good habits like prayer and reading the Bible in time of weakness strengthen resolve. Rely on God in times of weakness. "For the sake of Christ, then, I am content with weaknesses, insults, hardships, persecutions, and calamities. For when I am weak, then I am strong" (2 Corinthians 12:10 ESV).

- Honor God not yourself: It's easy to lose site of the goal when you score a touchdown, land a promotion, or receive a 100 percent on a test. Instead of celebrating your success, learn God's plan for your life through the experience. Does success direct your path or are you consumed by it? "One's pride will bring him low, but he who is lowly in spirit will obtain honor" (Proverbs 29:23 ESV).

- Remember, it's a marathon not a sprint: Moving full speed will quickly burn out anyone. No matter the physical shape or mental fortitude, a frantic pace cannot last. In ministry, the same can apply. Success in one venture may not point to the path you are supposed to travel. Study the big picture to understand the will of God for your life.

Life will be tough. You will face difficulties you won't understand and wonder how to persevere. Stay strong and seek victories that direct your path.

"If you don't like the result, you have to do something different," said Frank. "It means you must be correct in what you say, be correct in what you hear, and trust in God. When you do that, it'll correct what you see and direct your path. I want to encourage people no matter what they face—whether it's drugs, marriage problems, or kids making mistakes—stay strong because through it all, God will use that to further the kingdom. Look toward the plan of the Manufacturer of everything, and that's God."

Frank understood the plan for his life. He practiced hard, played like he practiced, and honors God today no matter the circumstance. Honor God in the plan He has for you.

DAY 18
GOD IS BIGGER THAN ALS

William White
Safety
Atlanta Falcons

By Del Duduit

Bless the LORD, O my soul, and forget not all his benefits,
who forgives all your iniquity, who heals all your diseases.
—Psalm 103:2–3 ESV

William White took on some of the roughest and toughest running backs in the NFL. After his successful career as a cornerback for the Ohio State Buckeyes, he played defensive back for the Detroit Lions and Kansas City Chiefs. And he also started Super Bowl XXXIII for the Atlanta Falcons.

He was known for his reputation as a fierce competitor on the gridiron and a leader in the huddle. But twenty years after he retired, he faced an onerous challenge.

He went for a check-up in Columbus, Ohio, when his doctor noticed his arm twitch. Tests revealed a disturbing diagnosis. His neurologist, a personal friend, had to share the difficult details.

"He came in and was crying and told me he had some bad news," he said. "He told me I had ALS (amyotrophic lateral sclerosis)."

William's response caught his buddy off guard.

"Okay. And?"

His doctor went on to stress the magnitude of ALS, also known as Lou Gehrig's disease.

"You are going to die," he told him. "There is no cure, and it is terminal."

But he took the news in stride and countered with two remarkable points:

"Everyone is born, and everyone is going to die. I can promise you God is not up there looking down and saying, 'Hmm, William, I didn't see that one coming.'"

In 2014, when the Buckeyes won the National Championship in football, the players celebrated and raised their arms in victory. The players did not think about training camp or practice—they were too busy enjoying the benefits of all of the months of hard labor and tribulations they endured to reach that moment.

"They got to where they wanted to be because of how hard they worked," William said. "This is how life is for me. I am going through a trial, and I know I'm going through this for a reason. I don't have to understand it all, but I do have to trust my Lord and Savior. He is bigger than my ALS. I can honestly say I'm not worried."

And we know that for those who love God all things work together for good, for those who are called according to his purpose.

—Romans 8:28 ESV

In the Huddle

Have you been given some tough news? Perhaps you received a grim diagnosis from your doctor. Maybe your spouse informed you she wants to separate. You might have a child on drugs, or maybe you just lost your job. People go through problems and trials every day. Have you ever wondered where God is in all this? How can good come from this mess? You are not alone. Many have felt this way before. But as a child of God, remember the Lord is always with you.

Cross the Goal Line

Just because you are a follower of the Lord does not meaning you are excluded from hardship. You do, however, have the best partner to help you cope. You have the Lord at your side to lean on in times of heartache. When your world is turned upside down by unexpected events, take into consideration these five ways to help heal your broken heart:

- Pray: God already knows what's happened in your life. He is a friend who is closer than a brother, so you can pour out your heart and rely on Him to listen and to calm your troubled spirit and give you peace. Sometimes when we don't even know what to say, Jesus can pray to the Father for us. Prayer strengthens your relationship with Christ and helps you to trust that His plan is for your good. Let Him know your heart's desires. "Ask, and it will be given to you; seek, and you will find; knock, and it will be opened to you" (Matthew 7:7 ESV). But what happens when the Lord doesn't answer your prayer in the way you expect?

You accept His answer. You are called to believe and have faith. Lean not on your own understanding.

- Get into the Word: God may have allowed you to face this trial because He wants to teach you an important lesson or get your attention. Study Scripture and look deep into His promises. "All Scripture is breathed out by God and profitable for teaching, for reproof, for correction, and for training in the righteousness, that the man of God may be complete, equipped for every good work" (2 Timothy 3:16–17 ESV). Inside, you will find the answers to your questions. Trust in His promises and seek His direction.

- Fast: When you sacrifice something important, you show Jesus Christ how serious you are. Most of the time when people fast, they give up food. But you might also forego an activity you enjoy such as golfing, fishing, or even checking social media. Remember it's not so much the actual act, but the Lord appreciates the sincere surrender of your heart as you remove distractions during a time you have set apart to focus on hearing from God. "Then you shall call, and the Lord will answer; you shall cry, and he will say, 'Here I am'" (Isaiah 58:9 ESV).

- Fellowship: Surround yourself with God's people to allow your pain and anguish to begin to ease. No one is exempt from problems and heartache, but companionship with your Christian brothers and sisters is a great way to cope, and they will offer you comfort, support, and love. Don't crawl into your shell, but rather open up to those who are close to you.

- Praise: No matter what you experience, give God the glory He deserves. You might ask yourself, "How can I worship God when my spouse died?" or "How can I give the Lord glory when I just found out I have cancer?" William did. After his horrible diagnosis, his attitude was to "accept and expect." He is excited to go to heaven. "I don't get to spend twenty, forty, or eighty years with the Lord," he said. "I get to spend an eternity with Him." If you can praise the Lord in bad times, you can do the same when life is good. Mighty things can happen when we trust God for His purpose. "For I know the plans I have for you, declares the LORD, plans for welfare and not for evil, to give you a future and a hope," (Jeremiah 29:11 ESV).

When you pray, read the Word, fast, fellowship, and praise, you will be well on your way to handle any crisis that comes your way. You will be able to tackle the biggest obstacle in your way when God is your safety.

DAY 19
IDENTITY

Samkon Gado
Running Back
Green Bay Packers

By Scott McCausey

What you have learned and received and heard and seen in me—practice these things, and the God of peace will be with you.

—Philippians 4:9 ESV

"You need to tell yourself you belong there. God put you in this position; you need to tell yourself that," said Coach Ken Karcher to his graduating senior Samkon Gado, who was just drafted by the Kansas City Chiefs. Samkon only started two games his senior season at Liberty University, yet his solid statistics and work ethic earned him an opportunity to play in the NFL.

"How can I play at this next level? They are going to find out I'm a fraud. They will discover I don't have huge stats," he said. "I didn't play at a big school where the competition was star-studded."

Yet Samkon was a playmaker, whether he started or came off the bench. He averaged more than five yards per carry every game at Liberty, and battered opponents with his north and south running style. The Chiefs saw this work ethic and signed him to a contract. He reported to mini camp and participated in all the drills and scrimmages.

Upon returning to campus, coach Karcher brought Samkon back to his office. "How do you think it went?"

"I think it went okay. I kept telling myself, I belong here," he said. " I played hard and gave it my best."

Coach Karcher interjected, "I just got off the phone with the Chiefs' coach. He said Samkon Gado was by far the star of rookie camp."

In the Huddle

There's an adage that says, "Practice like you play, because you'll play like you practice." Many former high school athletes look at quotes like this and wish they could go back in time. They didn't take practice seriously or maybe they counted the minutes until practice was over. Once the games began, they forgot their assignments, missed blocks, or ran in the wrong direction after the ball was snapped. Were you one of those people?

When it comes to faith, if you skate through life without opening the Bible or pursuing God through prayer, do you really have a priority in Jesus? "So flee youthful passions and pursue righteousness, faith, love, and peace, along with those who call on the Lord from a pure heart" (2 Timothy 2:22 ESV).

Practice can seem boring due to the repetitive nature. Plays are run over and over until every player performs their assignments flawlessly. But by the tenth time the same play is repeated, players start to grumble, and their minds begin to wander. Then the coach gets angry and orders sprints—the vicious cycle begins again. In the end, either the play has been perfected or a wedge has been driven into the team. Do you have the proper attitude in practice, understanding the goal? "Whatever you do, work heartily, as for the Lord and not for men, knowing that from the Lord you will receive the inheritance as your reward. You are serving the Lord Christ" (Colossians 3:23–24 ESV).

Cross the Goal Line

The team won't cross the goal line if they can't work together. Practice is the only way to ensure touchdowns. When we practice our faith, we lead others to the knowledge of Christ effectively. Here are some practical tips to remind you of the importance of practice.

- Instill healthy habits: The first time a new play is being tried, it is walked through. Everyone moves through their assignments in slow motion at the same time, revealing simple mistakes that seem almost silly. The mistakes are pointed out and the play is run again. As the play forms correctly, the tempo increases until it's run at full speed. The more you do something, the better you become. This might seem boring, but it's required for success.
- Avoid grumbling: The coaches realize practice drills and exercises are boring. They also understand players grumble when their bodies are subjected to the same arduous tasks at practice every day. Players must accept that the repetitive drills build muscle groups that prepare them for game day. Instead of wasting energy on complaining and sarcastically poking fun at the method of the coach's madness, hard work will improve skills and make the best use of time. "Do all things without grumbling or disputing, that you

may be blameless and innocent, children of God without blemish in the midst of a crooked and twisted generation, among whom you shine as lights in the world, holding fast to the word of life, so that in the day of Christ I may be proud that I did not run in vain or labor in vain" (Philippians 2:14–16 ESV).

- Know the goal: Do you know what you are playing for? Samkon understood the only way he would have a chance to make the Chiefs' roster was to work as hard as he could in mini camp. Failure was not an option to achieve the goal. When you see the goal in sight, honor God with your skill and make it a reality. "Commit to the Lord whatever you do, and he will establish your plans" (Proverbs 16:3).

- Work as a team: Accomplishing individual goals helps the team flourish. But each teammate relies on and helps one another to grow and improve. "Two are better than one, because they have a good reward for their toil. For if they fall, one will lift up his fellow. But woe to him who is alone when he falls and has not another to lift him up!" (Ecclesiastes 4:9–10 ESV).

- Get back up: You might lose a battle, but there's a war still to fight. If your opponent beats you on a play, learn from the defeat and try again. The answer is not to quit but to honor God. The disciples were often whipped, jailed, and ridiculed for their belief in Jesus Christ, but that didn't stop them. Use this as motivation to continue the pursuit in practice. "For whatever was written in former days was written for our instruction, that through endurance and through the encouragement of the Scriptures we might have hope" (Romans 15:4 ESV).

"I was blown away that the coach had this opinion. That entire year I had to keep pinching myself. This was really happening." Samkon said.

He continued to work hard. He was released by the Chiefs because they could not find a roster spot for him. But Samkon's determination on the practice team was recognized by the Green Bay Packers, and by God's providence, he was signed to a deal. Hard work in practice earns victory.

DAY 20
BE DIFFERENT

Vinny Rey
Linebacker
Cincinnati Bengals

By Del Duduit

But ye are a chosen generation, a royal priesthood, an holy nation, a peculiar people; that ye should shew forth the praises of him who hath called you out of darkness into his marvelous light.

—1 Peter 2:9 KJV

Vinny was seven years old when he gave his life to the Lord. Although he was young, he felt the need to be a follower of Christ.

His father was a role model for him in Far Rockaway, New York, and drove the A train in New York City for twenty-six years. "My dad was grateful and consistent and a hard worker," Vinny said. "He has character and integrity and taught me to have the same."

He honored his parents and tried to please them. He was obedient and did what they asked him to do. But when he was about fifteen years old, he gained a new perspective on life as a believer.

A contemporary Christian hip-hop group called The Cross Movement came to his church and had a tremendous impact on the teenager.

"It was really cool to hear them and meet them," he said. "I related to them and their message of Christ."

He related to this group of rappers who looked like him and dressed the same as he did. But there was something special about them. "They spoke like I did, but they were different," he added. "They were mature Christians who I related with and looked up to and wanted to be like."

From that point forward, he gained confirmation that he could still retain his identity and be different from the world at the same time. He could talk and dress the same as his schoolmates, but he did not have to partake in the same activities. He could let his light shine in a different way, and he liked how that felt.

> And be not conformed to this world: but be ye transformed by the renewing of your mind, that ye may prove what is that good, and acceptable, and perfect, will of God.
> —Romans 12:2 KJV

In the Huddle

You are a Christian and have some issues with worldly activities. You want to do what is right and please God, and at the same time, you want to have fun with your friends. Rest assured you can, as long as you distinguish good from evil. You must use proper judgment and adhere to limitations and convictions when it comes to your activities. Perhaps your buddies know you are a Christian and invite you to party at a bar late at night. Or they want you to go to a place where you know deep in your spirit that a follower of Christ should not go. As the old adage goes, "Never wrestle with pigs. You both get dirty, and the pig likes it."

Cross the Goal Line

At the risk of alienating your friends, you must make the decision to defend your convictions and be a good example for the kingdom. Once you lower your standards to please others, you in fact let them down. Here are some do's and don'ts for how to be different in the eyes of your friends:

- Don't compromise: Your friends and family have expectations of you as a Christian and may test you to see if you have the goods. If you give in, you will let them down and injure your reputation as a follower of the Lord. Take a stand.
- Don't judge: No one likes to be told they are wrong. If you condemn others for their behavior, you set a bad tone. Instead, let them know your personal beliefs about an issue without a judgmental attitude. For example, if you are invited to a poker night and you have convictions against gambling, simply thank them and pass on the offer. You might say, "Thanks for the invitation. But I won't be able to come because I personally don't gamble. This is just a conviction I have as a Christian. You guys have fun, and maybe next time I can do something else with you." Then you can invite them to church. "Judge not, and ye shall not be judged: condemn not, and ye shall not be condemned: forgive, and ye shall be forgiven" (Luke 6:37 KJV).
- Love them: When you show genuine concern for your friends, they will in turn respect you even though your decisions may be different. "Beloved, let us love one

another: for love is of God; and every one that loveth is
born of God, and knoweth God" (1 John 4:7 KJV).

- Encourage them: Lift others up with words of inspiration,
  and show them you believe in them to do what is right.
  Be a positive role model for Christ, and make sure others
  know that no matter what has happened in their past, Jesus
  loves them, you love them, and God will forgive, cleanse,
  and heal their broken heart and give them another chance
  in life.
- Pray for them: Prayer is the best thing you can do for anyone. Listen to the Holy Spirit, and show others how much
  you care about their happiness and their future. Tell them
  in love and friendship that they are in your thoughts and
  prayers. Let the Lord lead you in how you approach them
  and hold to your standards. "I exhort therefore, that, first
  of all, supplications, prayers, intercessions, and giving of
  thanks, be made for all men" (1 Timothy 2:1 KJV).

Set yourself apart and make a distinction between you and the
world. "Everyone else does it" is not a good reason for you to
turn away from what you know is right. Listen to your heart,
and if you feel the Holy Spirit telling you something is wrong,
please listen. You are a child of the King, so don't lower your
standards to be like everyone else. You are royalty. You are peculiar. You are different. Just because you live in this world of sin
doesn't mean you have to participate in sinful activities. Vinny
found alliances when the Christian group came to his church.
He found out he could be similar to his friends yet share a new
message of hope, show them a different way, and display his
love for Christ. Be a unique and effective witness for the Lord.

DAY 21
WHO ARE YOU?

Gerald McCoy
Pro-Bowl Defensive Tackle
Tampa Bay Buccaneers

By Cyle Young

Therefore, if anyone is in Christ, he is a new creation. The old has passed away; behold, the new has come.
—2 Corinthians 5:17 ESV

Gerald McCoy was accustomed to starting in football. At all ages, he played on the first-string lineup. In high school in 2005, he was named the *USA Today* Defensive Player of the Year and the Oklahoma Gatorade Player of the Year.

But when he arrived at the University of Oklahoma, he became a redshirt freshman. This status was not a big deal to him because it is common practice for most university football programs. The move paid off because he was later a two-time first team All-American and a two-time first team All-Big 12.

In 2010, the Tampa Bay Buccaneers selected Gerald as the third pick in the first round of the NFL Draft.

But in his rookie season, he tore his bicep and had to watch from the sideline while he recovered. The next year, he tore his other bicep.

The much-touted player was injured in back-to-back seasons.

"What's going on here?" he asked the Lord. "Why is this happening?"

No answer.

He repeated the question to God over and over.

Crickets. No answer.

He started to pose different questions to the Master.

"Who are You? Are You real?" he asked. "And who am I?"

Then it happened. The answer came to him and smacked him harder than one of his own crushing tackles. Gerald's priorities were out of sync. He had spent so many years with a focus to make it to the NFL, he had put God on the bench.

"That is when I realized I had to get my relationship right with the Lord," he admitted. "From that moment, I put God first in my life in everything. I knew better but got preoccupied. Ever since, I've had this peace about me that I don't ever want to lose."

Then his identity came back to him.

"I'm a football player," he realized. "That's who I am. That's who He called me to be. I'm a Christian football player!"

From that moment, he flourished by making appearances in six Pro Bowls and being named to three All-Pro teams.

For we are his workmanship, created in Christ Jesus for good works, which God prepared beforehand, that we should walk in them.

—Ephesians 2:10 ESV

Huddle Up

Life can become busy in a hurry. A new job can dominate your time. Then kids can come along and throw your life into a fun and crazy tailspin. Instead of doing what you once enjoyed, like a peaceful round of golf or fishing, you now sit and watch ballet practice or help prepare a baseball field for a Little League game. All is good, but you can get side tracked easily. Priorities can shift on a dime if you are not careful. You can be pulled in numerous directions and lose focus of what is important. Then all of a sudden, life may begin to unravel. Events you never anticipated or desired make an entrance into your world. Illness, job loss, or relationship issues can cause you to become distracted with your goals in life. Circumstances can make you feel lost or even make you question the Lord. Has this ever happened to you?

Cross the Goal Line

When your life does not turn out the way you imagined, how do you cope with the challenges? To question the Lord is human and natural. Your kids might question you if they don't understand a situation or the reason you made a certain decision. When you respond, you expect them to accept your answer. God does too. But when life moves fast, you may find it easy to lose focus. The Lord doesn't want to be put on the back burner and only be called on in a time of crisis. Keep Him on the first team at all times. Here are some of the top distractions and tips to keep them from becoming a priority:

- Money: Income is a must for survival. But you don't have to shift all your time and energy to obtain everything you can. You can become so obsessed with chasing the almighty dollar that you lose focus on what is important. Decide what you need, and hold steady. "For the love of money is a root of all kinds of evils. It is through this craving that some have wandered away from the faith and pierced themselves with many pangs" (1 Timothy 6:10 ESV). Money is not evil. But love of money can be a detriment.

- Routine: Redundancy can make you lose appreciation for all the magnificent things the Lord puts in your life. Take a different route to work one day, or take the family off for a spur-of-the-moment getaway. Mix up your schedule. Don't be so regimented that you can't go out of our way or take time out of your day to help someone in need or simply be available to a loved one.

- Work: You are obligated to your employer for a certain number of hours per week and then some. Or you may have your own business to try to keep afloat. There are times when your occupation might demand more of your time, and that is okay. But in the end, your boss or your coworkers will not be the ones who take care of you when you are ill. And they are not the ones excited to see you come home. Don't live to work; instead, work to live. Set boundaries.

- Hobbies: We all need creativity and recreation in our lives. You may enjoy golfing, fishing, boating, or writing. But don't let these take priority over your family. Allow your spouse and your kids to share in your experiences.

- Self: Put your faith and family first. Take care of yourself so you can take care of them, but make them a priority in all you do.

Here are some priorities to focus on instead.

- Family: Your parents, spouse, or children are some of God's richest blessings. Treasure every moment you have with them. "Behold, how good and pleasant it is when brothers dwell in unity" (Psalm 133:1 ESV).

- Church and friends: Fellowship with others makes your life more fulfilling. "Beloved, let us love one another, for love is from God, and whoever loves has been born of God and knows God" (1 John 4:7 ESV).
- Service to others: Help those in need, and you will be blessed every time. "Whoever brings blessings will be enriched, and one who waters himself will be watered" (Proverbs 11:25 ESV).
- Prayer and praise: Show honor to the Lord, and you will draw closer to Him. "Continue steadfastly in prayer, being watchful in it with thanksgiving" (Colossians 4:2 ESV).
- Time: Put God first on your schedule each day. Then focus on family, church, and work—in that order. "But seek first the kingdom of God and his righteousness, and all these things will be added to you" (Matthew 6:33 ESV).

When Gerald discovered life was not all about himself and finally got his priorities straight, he started to live up to his potential. When life comes to a halt, stop and consider what is important to you. Thank the Lord for all the gifts He has given you, and focus on what He wants you to be. Who are you? You are a child of the King!

DAY 22
STAY HUMBLE

Andy Dalton
Pro-Bowl Quarterback
Cincinnati Bengals

By Del Duduit

I therefore, a prisoner for the Lord, urge you to walk in a manner worthy of the calling to which you have been called, with all humility and gentleness, with patience, bearing with one another in love.

—Ephesians 4:1–2 ESV

Andy Dalton can be described in several ways. Tough. Relentless. Leader. Winner. Husband. Father. Athlete. Quarterback. Loyal.

But if you ask the six-foot-two, 220-pound signal caller, he might refer to himself as humble or thankful.

The multiple pro-bowler has played for the Bengals his entire career. He has set numerous team records, including 4,293 passing yards in 2013. That same year, he threw the most touchdowns in a season when he tossed thirty-three.

Success has come his way both on and off the field. Not only is he popular with the fans, but he and his wife Jordan operate the Andy and Jordan Dalton Foundation, which helps out families and children in need.

Yet, he is grounded in his faith and holds strong to his favorite verse: "Humble yourselves, therefore, under the mighty hand of God so that at the proper time he may exalt you" (1 Peter 5:6 ESV).

"It's not about me at all," he said. "It's all about glorifying God. It's about my wife and kids, and it's about my team."

He walks the walk and talks the talk.

There is no room for pride in his life. He has a family to raise, touchdowns to throw, and games to win. He honors the Lord and puts his own personal needs last.

"If I can put Jesus first and allow Him to work in me, then I'll be okay," he said. "That is how I was taught, and that's what I've experienced."

He echoes this message when he gives inspirational speeches to youngsters. "Find a good role model and get involved with a church group," he tells them. "A strong person of faith can be a great example of inspiration to a teenager." He also emphasizes how important it is to read God's Word every day. "I have to," he said. "It keeps me going."

His priorities are in focus, and he knows if he places the Lord first, his family second, and himself last, he will win life's Super Bowl.

> Do nothing from selfish ambition or conceit, but in humility count others more significant than yourselves.
> —Philippians 2:3 ESV

In the Huddle

You might be in a situation where you become arrogant. Perhaps you landed a promotion along with a big raise. You have the perfect "trophy" wife, and your children are wonderful in your eyes. You have it all. Your friends fight to spend time with you, and you are on top of the world. You are human, and you like to receive success and attention. Who doesn't? But keep in mind, you can fall just as fast as you rise to the top. If you become a snob to others, your life will change. When you need friends, they will not be around. When you ask for help, you will only hear crickets. Be careful not to think more of yourself than others and alienate those who have helped and prayed for you along your journey.

Cross the Goal Line

A humble heart reaps the most rewards. Do not use meekness to get what you want—strive to make it second nature. Don't confuse modesty with low self-esteem. In fact, it's just the opposite. Humility is defined by man as a modest or low view of one's own importance. Here this is what the Lord says about humility: "When pride comes, then comes disgrace, but with the humble is wisdom" (Proverbs 11:2 ESV). That's a better description. Here are some tips on how to stay humble in your walk with the Master:

- Know who is in charge: You would not have anything if it weren't for the mercy of Christ. "LORD, you have been our dwelling place in all generations. Before the mountains were brought forth, or ever you had formed the earth and the world, from everlasting to everlasting you are God" (Psalm 90:1–2 ESV). This sums it up pretty well, but the next time you get puffed up, I recommend you read the rest of Psalm 90.

- Serve others: Make a point to volunteer at a homeless shelter or work at a soup kitchen once a month. Don't look down at those in need, but rather help with a servant's heart. "For the Son of Man came not to be served but to serve, and to give his life as a ransom for many" (Mark 10:45 ESV). Just think, the King of kings sacrificed His life. You can give a couple of hours a month.

- Examine your own faults and ways to improve: Don't focus on the flaws of others. Recognize areas of opportunity to improve, make adjustments, and move on. Andy has to do this in the huddle or when he throws an interception. If he dwells on his mistakes, he is of no value. Stay in the pocket and continue to fire down field.

- Never draw attention to yourself: A good leader will deflect attention to others. Andy puts his team first all the time. When he connects for the game-winning touchdown, he will celebrate, but he always gives his offensive line and receivers the credit. You must do the same in order to foster a close-knit family. You will experience wins and losses. Lift up your wife and children in times of happiness and encourage them in times of sorrow. This also applies to your personal worship. Never praise God openly to show others how holy you are. Focus on Jesus and how good He has been to you and your loved ones. Worship Him in sincerity and truth. Make it personal—when you praise the Lord in His house, it is between you and Him.

- Ask the Father to help you stay humble: Pray He will help you stay focused on what is important. "The reward for humility and fear of the LORD is riches and honor and life" (Proverbs 22:4 ESV).

If you ask Andy what he wants to accomplish in his career, he will tell you he wants to win the Super Bowl. That is every football player's ambition. But if he ever gets to that mountain high, I expect him to recognize his team and his supporters who helped him reach this pinnacle. A true leader will exalt those around him and try to make them better. But his main focus is on his family. This is why Andy's foundation helps people and why he is admired in The Queen City. Set aside man's view of humility and concentrate on how the Lord sees it. "Before destruction a man's heart is haughty, but humility comes before honor" (Proverbs 18:12 ESV). Stay humble. You will be a sure-fire winner every time.

DAY 23
YOU SET THE EXAMPLE

Ben Roethlisberger
Super Bowl Champion Quarterback
Pittsburgh Steelers

By Del Duduit

> Be kindly affectionate to one another with brotherly love,
> in honor giving preference to one another; not lagging in
> diligence, fervent in spirit, serving the Lord.
> —Romans 12:10–11 NKJV

Ask yourself this question: Do you want your children to be like you?

Next question: Do you want your children to be like you when nobody is around?

Every father wants his offspring to be more successful than he was. But in what capacity? More money? A better career? More recognition?

This is what most men desire. But what do children want?

A dad who has all the money in the world? A father with a job that demands his time and takes him away from home?

I believe most children will tell you they want an example to follow. A man to look up to who will teach them right from wrong. A dad to take them to baseball practice and help them with their homework.

"I hope and pray I can have half the relationship with my kids that I had with my dad growing up," Ben Roethlisberger said. "With my children, they make me strive to be the best father and husband I can be. I have a huge responsibility, and I can't let them down."

The two-time Super Bowl champion quarterback enjoyed a wonderful childhood with a father who set the example. Ben's father took him to church and made sure the future All-Pro had a solid understanding of the Lord.

"He is a godly man and an amazing father and husband. So I strive to be half the man he is because there is no way I can be like him," he added. "He is as good as they come."

For Ben, he has experienced ups and downs in the NFL. He won the biggest game in the league and also tasted defeat. While he takes his job seriously as the leader of the Pittsburgh Steelers, his values are focused on a higher call to be the leader of his home.

He is determined to provide his children with a similar upbringing to the one he had in Lima, Ohio. This includes taking them to church to introduce them to Christ.

"My faith means everything to me," he said. "I play for His glory. He comes before football and before my family. I give God all the praise and glory because He has blessed me with an ability not too many people have, and I am so blessed to be able to share it. I want my kids to put the Lord first too."

> Be of the same mind toward one another. Do not set your mind on high things, but associate with the humble. Do not be wise in your own opinion. Repay no one evil for evil. Have regard for good things in the sight of all men.
>
> —Romans 12:16–17 NJKV

In the Huddle

All parents want the best for their children. Some achieve this, and others don't. Kids need a strong moral example and long for a man to lead them down the right path.

At other times, a career gets in the way and children are neglected. Perhaps one of the saddest songs ever sung is "Cat's in the Cradle" by Harry Chapin. The lyrics describe a father's unkept promises to spend time with his child while he puts his job first. Does your child long for your attention? Providing for your loved ones is essential, but this should never come before your obligation as a father. The family is the main target of the devil.

Cross the Goal Line

You want to teach a good work ethic to your children. But do you find yourself away too much at night? Do you check your email while you're with your son at baseball practice? Do you take care of business on the family vacation? If so, something needs to change. Put yourself in your kids' shoes. What was important to you when you were young? Your children need the following from you:

- Show them the love of Christ: If your main priority is to show them God, show them love first. Spend time with them and let them know they are the most important people in your life. Allow them to see God's love through your actions. "Therefore be imitators of God as dear children. And walk in love, as Christ also has loved us and given

Himself for us, an offering and a sacrifice to God for a sweet-smelling aroma" (Ephesians 5:1–2 NKJV).

- Demonstrate consistency: Be there for them when at all possible. Cut the meeting short to get to that game or recital. Eat dinner together and make time for regular family activities. This doesn't mean you have to cater to every interest, but help your kids develop skills that will assist them in life. Give praise when deserved and correction when needed.

- Make rules and keep them: Kids will push you to the limit, but if you establish boundaries and enforce them, they will appreciate them and follow your lead. This is often unpopular, but you will earn their respect. Do not give in, and be sure to hold true to your standards. You will get complaints, but deep down, your children will appreciate your care and concern for their safety and welfare. A no means just that. Sometimes you must use tough love, but love prevails. Don't be a tyrant but be stern. "Now no chastening seems to be joyful for the present, but painful; nevertheless, afterward it yields the peaceable fruit of righteousness to those who have been trained by it" (Hebrews 12:11 NKJV).

- Set a strong example: Your kids will watch you, even at times when you might not realize it. Children hear the way you talk to their mother, your friends, and your pastor. The old adage holds true: Monkey see, monkey do. And their imitations of you often make an appearance at inappropriate times. Does that make you feel uneasy or proud?

- Let the light of God shine through you: What your kids see when you worship the Lord or hear when you pray for them at night will stay with them and influence them to seek Christ. If they wander from the Cross, try not to get discouraged. Stay the course. Show them how wonderful it can be to serve the Lord. Don't force the issue, but let them observe Christ through you. Make your home an environment that will show them the way to heaven. Take them to church, whether they feel like it or not. You are the parent.

Ben enjoyed the blessings of being raised in church. He had a father who loved him and showed him the way to happiness. But Ben had to make his own personal decision to follow Christ. Ben's father set the example, and his son followed. Make it your goal to have the same impact on your son. You don't have to win a Super Bowl to be super dad.

DAY 24
FIND YOUR ASSURANCE

John Harbaugh
Super Bowl Winning Coach
Baltimore Ravens

By Del Duduit

Truly, truly, I say to you, whoever hears my word and believes him who sent me has eternal life. He does not come into judgment, but has passed from death to life.

—John 5:24 ESV

Super Bowl XLVII winning coach John Harbaugh summed up a football season in the NFL when he said, "It's like a life in a career that culminates in one season. There are so many things that happen during a season."

The NFL regular season is long enough at seventeen weeks. When you toss in the pre-season and post-season games, it adds up to nearly six months of football.

If a team gets off to a fast start and wins two or three games, all is good. But when the opposite happens, there could be a forecast for a long year.

"Every single week you can experience some of the highest highs and biggest triumphs," he said. "Then the next week, you can have a tough blow and experience one of the worst weeks ever. It can be a roller coaster of emotions."

But John, who has been at the helm for the Ravens since 2008, has one area of his life in control. His faith does not waver.

"My trust in God doesn't change; it keeps me grounded," he said. "I know that through it all, He's going to take care of me."

He knows God is with him no matter what he faces. He is there when his team wins and when it loses. God is present in laughter and even when the coach argues with a referee over a blown call.

"I basically pray throughout the whole game, not in the physical sense, but I have a prayerful mind and spirit," he said. "I pray a lot for the safety of all these guys all the time."

On the rare occasion when John gets in the flesh, because football is an emotional and violent game, he checks himself and comes back to reality.

"I have a sense about when things might tend to get away from me," he said. "I just have to come back and say, 'Hey, God, grab me; grab me here and pull me back.'"

He said he finds his true strength through his wife, his prayer time, and reading God's Word. "I have to read the Bible every day," he said. "I find my assurance there. When life gets crazy during the season, I know I find truth in there, and it always makes me calm."

His philosophy is to prepare each day to reach another level, both on the field and in his heart. "I have to get ready because I'm not there yet. That's why I pray and why I read the Bible. I want that assurance He gives me."

Do not be slothful in zeal, be fervent in spirit, serve the Lord.
—Romans 12:11 ESV

Huddle Up

Do you face circumstances of highs and lows like John does? Just because you are not a coach in the NFL does not exempt you from the experience of thrilling victories and costly defeats. You might go through a valley no one even knows about or have a joyous experience only you and your wife are aware of at the time. In either case, there has to be one constant in your life. You have to know you are a child of the King and are on your way to heaven. Do you know that?

Cross the Goal Line

Every now and then, especially in times of discouragement or trials, doubt may creep into your mind—this is a blitz from the devil. You need to know God cares about you, but you may still question it at times. If you are saved and live for the Lord, count your blessings. But it's also good to know He is with you at all times. Here are some ways to find confidence in your relationship with Christ and know you are on His team.

- Confession: Once you express your sin to the Lord and ask Him to come into your life, He will give you peace. "For God so loved the world, that he gave his only Son, that whoever believes in him should not perish but have eternal life" (John 3:16 ESV).
- Change: If you no longer talk the way you used to talk and go to the same places you once visited when you were a sinner, you know the Savior is in control. If you profess salvation but nothing changes, you need to reevaluate. "Therefore, if anyone is in Christ, he is a new creation. The

old has passed away; behold, the new has come" (2 Corinthians 5:17 ESV). When people see a change in you, you know you are on the right track. Put your past sins behind you, and ask God to give you strength to fight the battle against Satan and the traps he lays to make you fall back into temptation.

- Compassion: When you give your heart to the Lord, you will have a desire to help others. You will want to be around those who share the same philosophy and have a similar spirit. Show love for one another, and avoid all bitterness and strife. Show your love for your fellow brother. "Finally, all of you, have unity of mind, sympathy, brotherly love, a tender heart, and a humble mind" (1 Peter 3:8 ESV).

- Action: Don't be content to be on the team. Get on the field and participate. Become involved in your local church, in a Bible study, or in a community-based charity that spreads the Word of God. You can support a ministry or take a mission trip. When a tool stays on the workbench, it will become rusty. When bread sits out too long, it becomes moldy. Get active in church, and be on God's first team. Don't allow the devil a chance to put thoughts in your mind that God does not love you.

When you confess your sins and ask the Lord to lead you, that is assurance.

When people can see a definite change for the better in your life, that is assurance.

When you show compassion and love for your fellow man, that gives you assurance.

When you glorify the Master in all you do, that is assurance.

Satan will attack you from all sides. If you are a child of the King, claim the assurance He gives you that one day you will be with Him in paradise.

DAY 25
FAITH THROUGH ADVERSITY

Kirk Cousins
Quarterback
Minnesota Vikings

By Scott McCausey

Trust in the LORD with all your heart, and do not lean on your own understanding.

—Proverbs 3:5 ESV

With just over one minute to play, the Michigan State Spartans were driving to tie or win a huge game at Notre Dame Stadium. Kirk Cousins was given his first career college start on the road against the Fighting Irish and had played a solid game. The Spartans were down 33–30 and had already missed on a couple scoring opportunities, but they were knocking on the door at the Notre Dame eighteen-yard line.

Kirk dropped back to pass as heavy pressure came from the right side of the offensive line. He fired a pass off his back foot toward his hot receiver B. J. Cunningham, but the Notre Dame defensive back darted in front to intercept the pass at the ten. As time ticked away, so did the Spartan's chances, and they dropped a tough game on the road.

"I played well that day, but as God would have it I threw that interception, which cost us the game, forcing me to listen to the sound of 80,000 people cheering for my failure. As I walked off the field that day, I didn't feel good, but I remember thinking a thought of gratitude that God was the foundation of my life and football was not. If it had been, and you begin throwing game-ending interceptions, the foundation begins to crumble. I was very grateful I made my faith the most important thing of my life and Jesus Christ wasn't going to change any time soon."

In the Huddle

Everyone faces trials of many kinds, but it's what we do with those trials that dictates our heart and shows the love of Christ. It would have been easy for Kirk to point fingers at his team-mates. Blame could have been placed on his offensive line that missed a block. A finger might have been pointed at B. J. for not breaking toward the ball. Kirk could have blamed Larry Caper for missing a sure touchdown the play before. Yet he didn't play the blame game; he was thankful Jesus Christ gave him the opportunity to play. How often do you stay positive in light of certain circumstances? It might be easier to cast a negative light on teammates underperforming around us, but is this what God would have us do? "Blessed is the man who remains steadfast under trial, for when he has stood the test he will receive the crown of life, which God has promised to those who love him" (James 1:12 ESV). We should take James's counsel, as Kirk did, to glorify God.

Cross the Goal Line

Competition can bring out the best and the worst in people. We must remind ourselves of the goal to display God's kingdom on earth. The following are some ways we can better achieve this together.

- Tough times will come: Being a Christian is hard. You will be tested at every turn and at unexpected moments. Being ready to face the trials can give us the right attitude to avoid depression. There's always a chance of losing the battle, but winning the war is the goal. Jesus told His disciples, "I have said these things to you, that in me you may have peace. In the world you will have tribulation. But take heart; I have overcome the world" (John 16:33 ESV). Jesus comforts with the reminder of His ultimate victory.

- Pressure produces resolve: The Bible teaches how high-pressure moments bring out the best in us. "Consider it pure joy, my brothers and sisters, whenever you face trials of many kinds, because you know that the testing of your faith produces perseverance" (James 1:2–4) The clock is always ticking toward the end of the game where victory hangs in the balance, but each time you face this, it'll make future trials easier. Don't wilt in the face of adversity; strive forward utilizing the skills God gives you to succeed.

- Failure doesn't mean defeat: Kirk reminds us we may feel bad in the moment, but take heart; there will be more chances to shine. "But as for you, be strong and do not give up, for your work will be rewarded" (2 Chronicles 15:7). There's always another game to play, another season ahead, another chance to give your best. Don't allow one loss or missed opportunity beat you. Learn from it to overcome the next trial.

- Don't give up: There's always another challenge around the corner. Bouncing back from a perceived loss may seem insurmountable, but it must be done. Imagine if Kirk quit football after that game. He wouldn't have led the Spartans to a Big Ten title the next year. He wouldn't have played in the first Big Ten Title game two years later, and he wouldn't be in the NFL today. Henry Ford once said, "When everything seems to be going against you, remember that the airplane takes off against the wind, not with it." "Blessed is the one who perseveres under trial because, having stood the test, that person will receive the crown of life that the Lord has promised to those who love him" (James 1:12).

- Learn from your defeat: Remember it's not about the defeat but what you do with it that matters. Even a one percent success can change the world. If we learn from our defeat, victory will come. So, go into your trials with the right attitude to strive for success. "An intelligent heart acquires knowledge, and the ear of the wise seeks knowledge" (Proverbs 18:15 ESV).

"Despite my failure on the football field that day, God had bigger plans for me," Kirk said. "He used that event to bring glory to Himself and through it, allowed me to be a starting quarterback. He had much better days ahead, as this was a testing ground to teach me lessons to have more success at Michigan State and beyond."

DAY 26
THE KEY IS TO LOVE YOURSELF

William White
Safety
Atlanta Falcons

By Del Duduit

You, my brothers and sisters, were called to be free. But do not use your freedom to indulge the flesh; rather, serve one another humbly in love.

—Galatians 5:13

The key to a life with Christ is to first love yourself. This is not to be confused with a lover of oneself. There is a difference. William White explained what distinguishes the two forms of self-love.

To be a lover of yourself is to be arrogant and conceited. When you are in love with who you are, you have a narcissistic personality. You believe the universe revolves around you.

However, to love oneself means you walk in the Spirit of the Lord and accept God into your life.

"When you walk in His presence, you will not fulfill the lust of the flesh and think you are the most important person," he said. "When Christ is with you and in you, then you get better every day."

Focus on what God has in store for you, and accept His will in your life. Then you will be able to find happiness.

In 2016, William, who played college football at The Ohio State University, was diagnosed with ALS, better known as Lou Gehrig's disease, which is terminal.

"I don't worry about all the stuff that's going on in my life because I know God is in total control," he said. "And as long as He is in control of William, then William will be okay."

He says it all comes down to love. He loves the Lord, his family, and himself.

"He didn't love me because I played for the Buckeyes or that I played in a Super Bowl," he said. "The Lord loves William—period. So why would I worry about something that is in God's hands?"

When you love yourself, you are able to embrace the grace of God more and what He has in store for you in the future.

Rather, as servants of God we commend ourselves in every way: in great endurance; in troubles, hardships and distress.
—2 Corinthians 6:4

In the Huddle

Are you caught up in your own personal life? Are you a lover of yourself? Are you able to differentiate between being a lover of oneself and loving yourself? The first relates to arrogance and selfishness while the latter is all about knowing your self-worth in Christ. Have you been told you are insignificant? Perhaps you were bullied when you were a child or were made to feel unimportant in a bad relationship. Maybe you suffer from depression and have low self-esteem.

Cross the Goal Line

No matter what caused you to think less of yourself, you can battle back and realize your potential through the love of Christ. God made you, and His plans for you are good. But you will not reach your true potential if you do not love what He created. If you struggle with self-worth, here are some ways to help you acknowledge God's love for you and His true purpose for your life.

- Forgive yourself for your sins of the past: "If we confess our sins, he is faithful and just and will forgive us our sins and purify us from all unrighteousness" (1 John 1:9). While it is important to ask God to forgive you, you must also extend mercy to yourself.
- Remember you are precious in the sight of the Lord: "Since you are precious and honored in my sight, and because I love you, I will give people in exchange for you, nations in exchange for your life" (Isaiah 43:4). God sent His son to die for you, and Zechariah 2:8 says you are "the apple of His eye."
- Be the unique person God made you to be: "For you created my inmost being; you knit me together in my mother's womb. I praise you because I am fearfully and wonderfully made" (Psalm 139:13–14). God made one you, and He created a purpose just for you. Give Him glory and live life to the fullest.
- Don't be afraid to ask for help: Talk to the Lord, and seek the advice of a trusted friend or pastor. People may not know you need their help unless you take action to bring your needs to their attention. "My help comes from the Lord, the Maker of heaven and earth" (Psalm 121:2).
- Spend time around those you love: Fellowship with your family and friends can put a smile on your face and give you a sense of belonging. "Speaking to one another with

psalms, hymns, and songs from the spirit. Sing and make music from your heart to the Lord" (Ephesians 5:19).

- Trust God's plan for you: "In their hearts humans plan their course, but the LORD establishes their steps" (Proverbs 16:9). Dreams and ambitions are normal and healthy, but be patient. Don't get ahead of God, and don't get in His way. Let Him lead you down the right path.

- Don't put yourself down: This is the strategy of the devil. He loves to make you feel you do not matter and there is no reason for your existence. But don't listen to him. He is a liar and the father of untruths. When you hear a voice say you are not worth anything, always know the source is Satan, because God will never tell you this. Rebuke the enemy in Jesus' name.

- Give yourself room to make mistakes: You will mess up at times. Don't give up when you blunder. Use your error as a lesson, and determine to never make the same mistakes again. Pick yourself back up, ask God for forgiveness, and move forward. God does not expect us to be perfect, and He is the father of second, third, and more chances.

- Be honest with yourself: Recognize your strengths and weaknesses, and trust God to open doors for you to learn and make the right adjustments. Strive to be the humblest Christian you can be. "For by the grace given me I say to every one of you: Do not think of yourself more highly than you ought, but rather think of yourself with sober judgment, in accordance with the faith God has distributed to each of you" (Romans 12:3).

- Praise God for your life: "Praise the LORD, my soul; all my inmost being, praise his holy name" (Psalm 103:1).

We are more than conquerors through Christ, but self must take a back seat. There is no room for your own agenda if it conflicts with God's plan. Realize your full potential and dedicate your life to serve the Lord. When you give everything to God, you will discover a love for yourself through the power of Jesus Christ.

DAY 27
SHUNNING THE SPOTLIGHT

Samkon Gado
Running Back
Green Bay Packers

By Scott McCausey

He leads the humble in what is right, and teaches the humble his way.

—Psalm 25:9 ESV

In Samkon Gado's rookie season with the Green Bay Packers, the injury bug hit the team hard. Their offensive line suffered losses, and the running backs were decimated. Najeh Davenport and All-Pro Ahman Green were lost for the season, and Samkon was called into duty. He responded with a vengeance, running for sixty-two yards and a touchdown in his first NFL game. One week later, he earned his first NFL start against the Atlanta Falcons and gained 103 yards and two more touchdowns. For a practice player who only started two games for Liberty University his senior year, Samkon was making the most of his opportunity.

He quickly became a feel-good story and gained notoriety around the country. Fantasy football fanatics picked up Samkon for their teams, and he struggled to keep life in perspective.

"I'd never dealt with this kind of notoriety before. In high school I did well, and people in my school would get excited.

In college I had a few good games but not to the level to which I was known outside the halls of Liberty," he admitted "But when you turn the TV on and hear your name being discussed on a national level, it made me nervous. It made me wonder if all this was as important as people were making it. For me it was just football. I'd not changed, the game hadn't changed, but where I was playing had."

Samkon's success continued. He tallied 111 yards and a touchdown against the Philadelphia Eagles, 75 yards and a touchdown against the Chicago Bears, and 171 yards and a touchdown against the Detroit Lions before being named Rookie of the Week for the second time. But the NFL often stands for "not for long," and Samkon suffered a season-ending injury.

In the Huddle

Having success on the playing field is one of the goals and draws attention to those around us. As a Christian, this stage is set to honor our Savior. Being mindful of our success to give God the glory honors Him and brings perspective. When you've enjoyed success, do you thank the Lord for it? Do you understand success can be fleeting with times of trial waiting in the wings? Are you flaunting the success to bring honor to yourself? It's time to cross the goal line to discover ways to best put success into perspective.

Cross the Goal Line

Success can be fleeting. One day you enjoy it, the next you suffer defeat. How you act in the face of both can either honor or dishonor the Lord. Understanding how to handle it can effectively minister to those around you.

- Be humble: No matter if you've won the Super Bowl or a scrimmage, being gracious in victory is of the most admirable character traits. Our abilities are given from God, and the ultimate victory has already been won. So if Jesus wins the day by granting our skills, shouldn't He be the one exalted? Coach John Wooden once said, "Talent is God-given. Be humble. Fame is man-given. Be grateful. Conceit is self-given. Be careful." "Humble yourselves before the Lord, and he will exalt you" (James 4:10 ESV).

- Celebrate the Lord: When victory is in your midst, how do you celebrate? It's okay to congratulate your friends and teammates, but the Bible gives excellent examples. "Then Miriam the prophetess, the sister of Aaron, took a tambourine in her hand, and all the women went out after her with tambourines and dancing. And Miriam sang to them: 'Sing to the LORD, for he has triumphed gloriously; the horse and his rider he has thrown into the sea'" (Exodus 15:20–21 ESV). As soon as the Israelites crossed the Red Sea, the Lord flooded the pursuing Egyptians and won the day. Miriam then celebrated by thanking the Lord. Examples aren't given of Moses high-fiving Aaron or taunting the slave masters; they celebrated God in song. Thank God for the victory.

- Shine for the Savior: Individual accolades can be flattering. It's fun to win an award or receive compliments. But imagine the joy God receives when our victories are given to Him. "For am I now seeking the approval of man, or of God? Or am I trying to please man? If I were still trying to please man, I would not be a servant of Christ" (Galatians 1:10 ESV). Evangelism takes place when you serve God in this way.

- Maintain a kingdom perspective: Jesus said, "Go therefore and make disciples of all nations, baptizing them in the name of the Father and of the Son and of the Holy Spirit, teaching them to observe all that I have commanded you. And behold, I am with you always, to the end of the age" (Matthew 28:19–20 ESV). We are given the command to share the good news with people who don't know it. Sports is a way to accomplish this, both within your team and outside it. The bigger picture is not a championship; it is the growth of God's kingdom.
- Get back to work: One truth about sports is you won't stay on top forever. Remember, your platform may be temporary, but use it to give God the glory. Continue to work hard, and don't settle for the moment.

"I thank God we have a Father in heaven who can see all thing and knows what is best for us," Samkon said. "When I was in that moment, I didn't understand as much as I do now. When Jesus Christ was on earth, there were so many times He could have made Himself more famous. Even to the point of His death you see Him shunning the spotlight. When I look back, I see this as more desirable. My NFL success served the purpose of giving me a story to tell later in life during my medical career."

Samkon continues to tell his story, which opens doors to share Jesus Christ. His career was short, but the impact of his humble play directs people to the Father.

DAY 28
A BIG OLE TEDDY BEAR

Benjamin Watson
Super Bowl Champion Tight End
New Orleans Saints

By Del Duduit

For God so loved the world that he gave his one and only Son, that whoever believes in him shall not perish but have eternal life.

—John 3:16

A stuffed teddy bear played a significant role in Benjamin Watson's salvation experience.

The rough and tough NFL tight end for the New Orleans Saints was five or six years old when he first came to his faith.

He and his family lived in Virginia Beach, and he always had a ritual of rolling around and wrestling with his teddy bear before he went to bed each night.

"Me and Dad usually play-fought with it before I went to sleep, and one night I remember, I fought the bear, and the bear won," he said. "I lost the fight, and I was upset. I remember sitting on my bed crying and asked my dad if we could fight him one more time because I wanted to win."

His father brought the stuffed animal back for a rematch. This time, Benjamin was victorious. After the epic battle, the young boy and his dad had a serious talk.

"We talked about winning and losing," he said. "He asked me what would happen if I died that night."

His father, a pastor, delivered a knockout blow to his boy.

"I didn't know the answer, and I grew up in church," he said. "Right there, I understood the gravity of my sin and my need for forgiveness."

Although Benjamin was a young child, he understood the seriousness of the moment. He said he felt separated from the Holy Spirit and knew he needed to be saved from his sin. His father read through John 3:16 and pointed the way to the Cross for his son.

"Over the course of my life, I still think back on the moment, and I'm thankful that at a young age, I was able to feel the conviction," he said.

Now he is a father and tries to lead his children in the same way he was directed.

"I want my kids to see God in me first," he said. "I hope one day they will make the same decision I made to follow the Lord. I can't do it for them, but I can show them love, honesty, and forgiveness. I want to be transparent and let my life glorify God in all I do."

If anyone speaks, they should do so as one who speaks the very words of God. If anyone serves, they should do so with the strength God provides, so that in all things God may be praised through Jesus Christ. To him be the glory and the power for ever and ever. Amen.

—1 Peter 4:11

Huddle Up

Do you remember when you were introduced to the Master? Is your conversion still fresh in your mind? If you cannot recall the specifics, it's okay. But have you truly experienced salvation? Maybe you grew up in church but have never felt conviction or His saving grace. Be aware you cannot depend on your parents' status or regular church attendance to get you into heaven. Do you have your own genuine, personal relationship with God?

Cross the Goal Line

Do you feel God's convicting power to change your life? Do you have a desire for everlasting life and to live in heaven with the Lord after you leave this world? Are you sick of sin and want to lead a godly life for your children? Do you want to be saved? There are not ten steps to salvation. The Word of God makes giving your heart to the Lord so simple that even a child can understand.

- Hear the Word: You must be exposed to the gospel of Jesus Christ. Salvation is not something you inherit from your family. *You* must make the decision. But in order to make a choice, you have to hear what God says. I encourage you to attend a Bible-believing church and listen to the truth. Once you've heard the plan of salvation presented, the next step is up to you. "For what I received I passed on to you as of first importance: that Christ died for our sins according to the Scriptures, that he was buried, that he was raised on the third day according to the Scriptures" (1 Corinthians 15:3–4).

- Believe: Here is the choice. You can accept or reject what you have heard. You can opt to trust that Christ is the risen Savior and follow Him, or you can turn your back on Him and serve the enemy. "Whoever believes and is baptized will be saved, but whoever does not believe will be condemned" (Mark 16:16).

- Repent: You must admit you are a sinner. This is not a ploy but rather reality. You have faults and have done wrong in God's eyes. You may live a good life and set a fabulous example, but your sins still need to be forgiven. "Repent, then, and turn to God, so that your sins may be wiped out, that times of refreshing may come from the Lord" (Acts 3:19).

- Confess: You must own up to your sins and ask the Lord for forgiveness. You must promise to walk in His footsteps and change your ways. "If you declare with your mouth, 'Jesus is Lord,' and believe in your heart that God raised him from the dead, you will be saved" (Romans 10:9).

- Trust: Live the life the Lord has provided for you. Attend church on a regular basis, pray every day, and spend time daily in the Word of God. "Trust in the LORD will all your heart and lean not on your own understanding; in all your ways submit to him, and he will make your paths straight" (Proverbs 3:5–6).

Once you make the decision to become a Christian, prepare to receive joy and happiness in your heart. You aren't promised a problem-free life, but you are guaranteed everlasting life. The Lord and your Christian friends will help you in your walk of faith. You will not be alone, and you will have peace and friendship like never before. And when the Lord wraps His arms around you, it will feel like you are hugging a great big loving teddy bear.

DAY 29
GOD CAN BURN OUT THE HATE

Chad Pennington
Quarterback
New York Jets

By Del Duduit

Cast your burden on the LORD, and he will sustain you; he will never permit the righteous to be moved.

—Psalm 55:22 ESV

Chad Pennington was a dependable quarterback in the NFL for several years. He was a quiet leader and a model of consistency on the field.

On November 16, 2003, he earned his way onto a rare list of quarterbacks who have posted a perfect passer rating. He went 11 of 14 for 219 yards and scored three touchdowns in a loss against the Indianapolis Colts. Twice he led the NFL in passing completion percentages, and in 2002, he was the NFL leader in passer ratings.

He also won the NFL Comeback Player of the Year two times and was named the Most Improved Player in 2002.

But deep down, he harbored a hatred that festered inside of him until he turned it over to the Lord.

For years, Chad devoted himself to the game of football. He was a college standout at Marshall University and an effective signal caller in the NFL. But the game was his god.

After a couple of surgeries and injuries, he was benched. He felt betrayed and hurt. The coaches and teams to which he had devoted his life and off-season time had turned their backs on him.

"The game I loved so much I now hated," he said. "It was a personal furnace, because I did not know how to handle it. I'd been loyal all these years, and now my coaches turned on me."

But God had a plan, although at the time, Chad did not see what He had in store.

"I had placed so much of my time on the game that once it was taken away from me, I felt like I was not of any value to anyone," he said. "I had no worth. I had no purpose anymore."

God started to work on him. The Master had the quarterback right where He needed him to be.

The game was burned out of him, and a new fire ignited— one that would allow him to help other players who go through identity issues once they leave the lavish lifestyle of the NFL.

"When who you are is taken away, it can have a big impact," he said. "Some of these guys retire or are released, and that's all they know. They struggle with who they are."

For some players, the limelight and adoring fans fuel their fire. When they depart the league, water is poured on their flames, and the lights go out.

No more autograph seekers. No more first-class treatment. No more interviews. All of the special attention is gone.

Chad faced this loneliness even before he retired, and he now consults with the NFL to help players adjust to life after football.

"My experience has helped me to relate and let them know there is something out there for them," he said. "I'm glad now that God let me see this before I left the league. God knew what He was doing but let me figure it out."

> But the Helper, the Holy Spirit, whom the Father will send in my name, he will teach you all things and bring to your remembrance all that I have said to you.
>
> —John 14:26 ESV

Huddle Up

Do you put an activity in front of God? Does your work take priority over your commitment to Christ? Perhaps your hobby is more important to you than your relationship with the Savior. Do you check work emails on a Sunday morning or do you attend church? Priorities in life can easily become jumbled and get out of line. Don't beat yourself up if you are pulled in many different directions. Rest assured, you are not alone. Take the time to make God your first priority.

Cross the Goal Line

Chad went through a valley so God could prepare him to help others who face similar challenges. He came out on top and now sees why he went through his ordeal. Appreciate God's blessings in life before you go through a life-altering situation. Whether you are laid off from your job or you choose to retire, you will have to adjust to what life throws at you. Are you prepared? Here are some ways to stay involved in the work of the Lord and keep your priorities in perspective:

- Put time with God on your calendar: This is a great practice, especially if you are a workaholic. Get into a routine, and don't let the world distract you. Make time for the Lord first thing every day. "But his delight is in the law of the LORD, and on his law he meditates day and night" (Psalm 1:2 ESV).

- Hold devotions every day: Invest in a solid Bible-based devotional, and connect with the Master. Get up early for prayer and Bible study. Morning is a good time for just you and God. Put your phone away, grab a cup of coffee, and spend time alone with the Lord.

- Stay in the Word: Be faithful to read God's Word each day. If you have a busy schedule and are always on the go, invest in an audio version of the Bible or find some podcasts by your favorite ministers to listen to on your commute. God's words of instruction are much more positive than the gloomy news on the radio. Listening to the Bible is also a great way to unwind on your way home. "It is written, 'Man shall not live by bread alone, but by every word that comes from the mouth of God'" (Matthew 4:4 ESV).

- Become involved in a ministry: Choose a charity or a ministry to spread the gospel. Write a blog or volunteer at church functions or work to help promote a social issue that is close to your heart and beliefs. The point here is to surround yourself with likeminded people. "Do your best to present yourself to God as one approved, a worker who has no need to be ashamed, rightly handing the word of truth" (2 Timothy 2:15 ESV).

- Rely on a partner: Join together with your spouse or a close friend who you can confide in, and hold each other accountable. Build a solid team around you, and march to victory.

Life can be great one day and get turned upside down the next. You might face a sudden job loss or the sickness of a family member. Be prepared, and don't allow the devil to catch you off guard. Turn all hate over to God before it has a chance to blindside you with a blitz.

DAY 30
HOW TO HANDLE PERSONAL
STRUGGLES

Tom Lamphere
Chaplain
Minnesota Vikings

By Del Duduit

> But if I know that what I am doing is wrong, this shows that
> I agree that the law is good. So I am not the one doing wrong;
> it is sin living in me that does it.
>
> —Romans 7:16–17 NLT

Everyone makes mistakes.

Everyone experiences a tragedy.

Everyone will struggle.

But it's how you respond in these times that defines who
you are.

Tom Lamphere witnessed all these battles during his
twenty-five-plus years as team chaplain for the Minnesota
Vikings.

"All of us will go through difficult times and face personal
turmoil," he said. "But how do we handle it? I think when we
open up as coaches and players, it helps to heal or get through
a challenge."

A couple examples come to mind. When Tony Dungy's son died in 2005 at the age of eighteen, Tom recalled how the Hall of Fame coach drew closer to the Lord to seek comfort for his wounds. He also referenced Ben Roethlisberger, who fought to get back to God after a time of intense trial.

"When people are in the spotlight and they profess Christianity, everyone watches to see how they respond to this type of event," he said. "People watch to see how they get through, and it's always through the grace of God."

Celebrities and professional athletes who are followers of the Lord seem to be under a microscope when they face personal issues. The world observes and judges them based on their reactions.

"I'm not sure if everyone is looking to see if they mess up or not, but they are looking to see if what they have is real. Is this Jesus thing real? Does it work?"

Life comes down hard on people, and chances are it will happen to you if it hasn't already. When you face the storms of life, you have many choices to make.

The Lord wants you to choose Him because He will provide comfort and a solution. The forces of evil want you on their side in order to destroy you.

"What road will they go down?" Tom said. "Will they choose drugs, alcohol, sex, or all the other stuff that doesn't help? These only make things more complicated, and they look at it as a quick fix."

The world wants to see if an athlete's walk with Christ is authentic or not.

"Some of our guys come under tremendous scrutiny. So I tell them, if you start talking about God, you had better be ready to show them it's real," he said. "Don't tell them you trust God and go out and get arrested for DUI. Live the life, and let God reward you."

> Thank God! The answer is in Jesus Christ our Lord. So you see how it is: In my mind I really want to obey God's law, but because of my sinful nature I am a slave to sin.
>
> —Romans 7:25 NLT

Huddle Up

How do you handle sticky situations? If you are like most people, you have experienced some form of problem, challenge, or tragedy. Some are easier to deal with than others. What might seem small to one person is giant to the one going through the valley. Everyone is wired differently and chooses to cope in their own unique ways. Perhaps you have been hit with a job loss or death of a relative. Maybe you received dreadful news from a doctor or found out you have lost your life savings. The devil wants you to give in and become angry. The human side says that's the best choice. Temptation is around every corner, but it will not help to give into it.

Cross the Goal Line

When life gets turned upside down and appears to crash all around you, this is the best time to call on the Lord. Drugs and alcohol are not the answer. On the other hand, you have to guard against depression and anxiety, which will lurk in the shadows and wait for your invitation. The Lord never promised a walk in a rose garden, but He did vow to take every step with you, even when you feel alone. Challenges can be met and you can overcome, but God must be the one you look to for guidance.

- Don't look at the size of your problem, but focus on the Lord's power: A wall can seem too high to climb at times, or the valley can be too low to cross. The Master promised to never leave or forsake us. He will be there for you, so look to Him for help. He is bigger than any mountain and is a cool drink of water in the valley. "Give all your worries and cares to God, for he cares about you" (1 Peter 5:7 NLT).

- Even when you don't understand, hold true to His plan: His plan might be tough to follow at times. You worked hard in life to get ahead, and all of a sudden, you face a huge mountain. Life might not be fair at times, especially when tragedy hits. No matter what you face, be ready to say yes to whatever the Lord asks of you. Depend on the Lord for guidance and assurance, and trust Him to reveal His plan to you. "Trust in the LORD with all your heart; do not depend on your own understanding" (Proverbs 3:5 NLT).

- Seek shelter with others: Talk with friends and members of your church who might have gone through similar situations and confide in them. Choose those who will be a source of comfort and go to the Father in prayer on your behalf.

- Do not force something to happen: God's plan is best. Find ways to occupy your thoughts, and focus your mind on heavenly issues. Become active in church functions or volunteer for community service. Find ways to encourage others. "Don't be selfish; don't try to impress others. Be humble, thinking of others as better than yourselves" (Philippians 2:3 NLT).

- Be prepared to rejoice: Be ready, because one day when you understand it all, you will glorify the Lord. A season of joy will come. Keep your eyes turned toward the sky and your heart pure. Trust Him to deliver you from your problems. Demonstrate patience and magnify His name while you wait. "Wait patiently for the LORD. Be brave and courageous. Yes, wait patiently for the LORD" (Psalm 27:14 NLT).

There are many other ways to handle stressful and unwanted circumstances. But the key is to let the Lord take over and get out of the way. This doesn't mean you don't do anything, it means to give way to the Holy Spirit. Lean on the Lord even if you don't feel Him near. Just like the poem, "Footprints in the Sand," the Master will carry you through the tough times. You will get through the pain and praise Him again.

ABOUT THE AUTHORS

Del Duduit is an award-winning writer and a lifelong resident of Southern Ohio. As a sports writer and former sports newspaper editor, he has won awards from the *Associated Press,* the Ohio Prep Sportswriters Association, and the Ohio News Network.

As a Christian writer, he is the author of *Buckeye Believer: 40 Days of Devotions for the Ohio State Faithful* and *Bengal Believer: 40 Who-Dey-Votions for the Cincinnati Faithful* (BY Books, 2019), and he earned the Outstanding Author award at the 2017 Ohio Christian Writers Conference, as well as two more first place awards. He was also published in *Faith and Freedom* (EA Books, 2018) and is a contributor to *The Serious Writer's Guide to Writing,* pending publication by Serious Writer Inc.

His articles have been published in *Clubhouse Magazine, Sports Spectrum, Bridges*, and *PM Magazine.* He is a coeditor and writer for Southern Ohio Christian Voice, and his articles have been published on One Christian Voice, ToddStarnes.com, The Sports Column, Almost An Author, and *The Write Conversation.* His weekly blog, *My New Chapter*, appears on delduduit.com, and he is a contributing writer for Athletes in Action and *The Christian View.* He is represented by Cyle Young of Hartline Literary Agency.

Follow Del on Twitter (@delduduit) and on Facebook (www.facebook/delduduit).

Del and his wife Angie are the parents of two adult sons, Gabe and Eli. They attend Rubyville Community Church.

Michelle Medlock Adams is an award-winning journalist and best-selling author, earning top honors from the *Associated Press*, the Society of Professional Journalists, and the Hoosier State Press Association. Author of more than seventy books with more than 1 million books sold, Michelle's book, *Love and Care for the One and Only You* (Worthy Inspired) was featured on the "Praise the Lord" program on TBN and "The Harvest Show" on the LeSea Broadcasting Network. She is the president of Platinum Literary Services and PlatLit Books.

Since graduating with a journalism degree from Indiana University, Michelle has written more than one thousand articles for newspapers, magazines, and websites; acted as a stringer for the *Associated Press*; written for a worldwide ministry; helped pen a *New York Times* bestseller; and served as a blogger for *Guideposts*. Today, she continues working as a TV host for TBN's "Joy in Our Town" and successfully running her own freelance writing business.

Michelle currently writes two devotions per month for Todd Starnes of Fox News at his website toddstarnes.com. She also blogs monthly for *Lift Up Your Day* and *Lift Up Your Day for Ladies*. You can learn more at www.michellemedlockadams.com. She is represented by Cyle Young.

Ryan Farr is a collegiate coach, speaker, and pastor whose goal is to reach lost families with the truth of Jesus Christ. Having participated in both football and lacrosse as a student at

Malone University, athletics have been a significant part of Ryan's walk, both in life and with the Lord—one of the root reasons for his passion for utilizing sports as ministry. For the past nine years, Ryan has been involved in coaching lacrosse (among many other sports) and local church ministry and is currently the head men's lacrosse coach at Mount Vernon Nazarene University (OH). Additionally, Ryan has been a part of creating All Out Sports, a sports ministry curriculum that promotes the skills of athletics as well as Bible lessons for young athletes. When not coaching, Ryan enjoys watching movies with his family, walks with his wife, and attending Youngstown State football games. Originally from Youngstown, Ryan now resides in Mount Vernon, Ohio, with his wife Rachel and three sons, Colton, Mason, and Easton.

Beckie Lindsey is an award-winning writer, poet, freelancer, and blogger. She is the author of the YA series Beauties from Ashes (Elk Lake Publishing) and is the editor of Southern California Voice, a division of One Christian Voice LLC, a national news syndicating agency. She is the author of devotions and a Bible study and is represented by Cyle Young, Hartline Literary Agency, and Tessa Hall is her junior agent.

Scott McCausey is the director of radio ministries at Christian Devotions Ministries. He interviews famous authors, Christian recording artists, renowned ministers and evangelists, sports celebrities, and special interest leaders each Tuesday night on Christian Devotions Speak UP! His program is also syndicated through Theology Mix ministries.

A former pastor, Scott is also the senior scientist at Eagle Design and Technology in Zeeland, Michigan. He's performed various duties throughout his twenty-seven-year career, and his vast knowledge of polyurethane allows him to answer difficult technical questions and steer new programs in the right direction.

Cyle Young is a multiple-genre award-winning author of more than sixteen writing awards. He considers himself a "binge writer" and routinely scribes thirty thousand words in a weekend. He finds great joy in writing and loves to bounce between crafting epic high fantasy tales, helpful nonfiction parenting books, and getting lost in the melodic rhythm of children's poetry.

As a former National Champion football player at the University of Michigan, Cyle takes pride that he won his first writing award for his princess picture book, *Princess Penelope*.

He serves as managing editor of www.almostanauthor.com, a website devoted to helping aspiring writers become published. He is also a monthly contributor to the parenting website, www.just18summers.com and is the co-owner of Series Writer Inc.

Cyle is a cowriter of All Out Sports devotionals and curriculums, used annually by more than ten thousand students and parents. He is a literary agent for Hartline Literary Agency. He and his wife Patty have three wonderful children on earth and two in heaven.

If you enjoyed this book, will you consider sharing the message with others?

Let us know your thoughts at info@ironstreammedia.com. You can also let the author know by visiting or sharing a photo of the cover on our social media pages or leaving a review at a retailer's site. All of it helps us get the message out!

Facebook.com/IronStreamMedia

———————————

Iron Stream Books is an imprint of Iron Stream Media, which derives its name from Proverbs 27:17, "As iron sharpens iron, so one person sharpens another."

This sharpening describes the process of discipleship, one to another. With this in mind, Iron Stream Media provides a variety of solutions for churches, missionaries, and nonprofits ranging from in-depth Bible study curriculum and Christian book publishing to custom publishing and consultative services. Through our popular Life Bible Study, Student Life Bible Study brands, and New Hope imprints, ISM provides web-based full-year and short-term Bible study teaching plans as well as printed devotionals, Bibles, and discipleship curriculum.

For more information on ISM and Iron Stream Books, please visit

IronStreamMedia.com

CPSIA information can be obtained
at www.ICGtesting.com
Printed in the USA
BVHW042000131221
623946BV00013B/1035

9 781563 092312